Hold Me Tightly

Hold Me Tightly

Devotions on a Mother's Love

by
Catherine Duerr

SAINT LOUIS

Copyright © 1996 Catherine Duerr
Published by Concordia Publishing House
3558 S. Jefferson Avenue, St. Louis, MO 63118-3968
Manufactured in the United States of America

Library of Congress Cataloging-in-Publication Data

Duerr, Catherine.
        Hold me tightly: devotions on a mother's love / Catherine Duerr.
        p.   cm.
        ISBN 0-570-04847-8
        1. Mothers—Prayer-books and devotions—English.   I. Title.
BV283.M7D84   1996
242`.6431—dc20   95-53344

2   3   4   5   6   7   8   9   10   05   04   03   02   01   00   99   98   97   96

TO THE GLORY AND HONOR OF GOD
and with love to our children,
Mark, Nicholas, and Angela

How great is the love the Father has lavished on us,
that we should be called children of God.
1 John 3:1

Contents

Hold Me Tightly

One Step at a Time

irst we have to put the butter in the bowl. Will you please unwrap it and put it in there? I will measure the sugar." Mark, my 3-year-old son, and I were seated on a towel in the middle of the kitchen floor, making brownies. "Now you can put the sugar in the bowl and stir it."

"I aw done 'tirring."

"Okay, let me stir it a little more. Can you crack the eggs in this bowl? Oh, oh! You don't have to crush the shell so hard. Oops."

We continued this process through the recipe, one step at a time. I enjoyed making the brownies with Mark. But I kept alert to stay a step ahead of him, so when he was ready to add the next ingredient, I had it measured and ready to go. I walked him through the brownie-making, step by step, helping with what he could not quite handle.

"Part of cooking is cleaning up afterwards. Will you please put the dishes in the sink and throw these wrappers away?" Mark completed his tasks and then sat down to lick the gooey, batter-covered spoon. I finished cleaning up.

When Daddy came home, the aroma of baking brownies filled the air. "What do I smell?" he asked.

Mark ran to hug Daddy. "I made brownies!"

"You made brownies? Wow, I'm impressed!"

Yes, Mark made the brownies, but I wonder what they would have tasted like or what the kitchen would have looked like without my help.

I, too, have help with many tasks. When I attempt to do something that seems beyond my abilities, God is there, getting the ingredients ready, guiding me through the steps, and cleaning up the messes I make. Through Jesus, He did something I could never do for myself—He forgave my sins. And He helps me live each day as His child. Sometimes I do not even realize how much He helps me along the way. But with God's help, the difficult and the impossible are within my reach.

Dear Father,

Thank You for being with me and helping me. When I start to think something is impossible, lead me through, step by step, taking care of what I cannot handle by myself. Support and strengthen me daily as Your child. Amen.

I can do everything through Him who gives
me strength.
Philippians 4:13

Jesus, Hold Me Tightly

icholas did not know what he was in for today. As the nurse readied the syringe, he sat on my lap, his big, green eyes taking in all the sights around him. I steeled myself against the pain as I positioned my hand on his pudgy leg, ready to hold it still. My fingers squeezed his soft fleshy thigh as the nurse plunged the needle deep into his leg. The needle was almost out when the pain registered in Nicholas' brain. His wide green eyes got bigger and then clenched shut as he screamed. As soon as the needle was out, I turned his body, wrapped my arms around him, and snuggled him to my breast. I pressed my cheek next to his, kissed the side of his face, and stroked his hair. He settled down, but all the way home he took long draws on his pacifier and stared at me. He seemed to be asking, "How could you?"

I knew that having Nicholas vaccinated against diphtheria was the right thing to do. That tiny little poke was nothing compared to the torture of the disease he might contract if he were not protected. It had hurt him, and his pain hurt me. But I comforted him, knowing the good that would result.

When I hurt, whether it be in little or huge ways, God is not callous to my pain. He is always right there to wrap His arms around me and comfort me, even when He allows me to experience the pain in the first place. Even while I'm in the midst of pain, He brings encouragement and blessing in Christ. He holds me tightly and promises me a new, pain-free life with Jesus someday.

Dear Father,

Please hold me until the pain passes. In Jesus' name. Amen.

Praise be to the God and Father of our Lord Jesus Christ, the Father of compassion and the God of all comfort, who comforts us in all our troubles, so that we can comfort those in any trouble with the comfort we ourselves have received from God.
2 Corinthians 1:3–4

Perfect Love

ark's shorts looked like he had scooted around the backyard on his bottom. But I had seen the mud on his shoes and figured that he must have walked at least a little bit to gather that much filth.

I opened the medicine cabinet and reached for the stain stick. I wanted to get as much of the grime out as possible before it could set. After thoroughly smearing the shorts with the stick, I tossed them in the hamper. I placed the cap back on my *deodorant* and started to return it to the medicine cabinet. I did a double-take. Oh, great, I just smeared deodorant all over Mark's shorts. No wonder it didn't glide on as easy as usual.

So I'm not perfect. This little incident does not bother me as much as some of the other blunders I have made. The worst that can happen here is that I ruined a pair of Mark's shorts. Even if they are permanently stained, he can still slide around the backyard on his bottom in them.

The mistakes that bother me more are the ones that hurt others. I regret the times that I have disciplined improperly, ran out of patience, or misjudged a situation and handled it poorly. I have made mistakes and will continue to do so.

Now I have written an entire book of devotions comparing my relationship with my children to God's relationship with me. Through this process, I was constantly reminded that I am not perfect. These devotions helped me focus on how much God loves me. He loves me like His child. That is something that I can understand because I know how much I love my children. And yet, God loves me even more than that.

God's love for me is flawless. He never loses His patience. He never disciplines improperly. He never misjudges. While looking at the love I have for my children can help me better understand God's love for me, it is only a start. God's love is so much greater and so much more perfect than anything I have to offer.

Dear Father,

Again and again I am reminded of Your magnificence. The love You have for me surpasses anything I can imagine. I do not even know where to begin to love like You do. I ask You to let Your love shine through me. Amen.

As for God, His way is perfect; the word of
the Lord is flawless. He is a shield for all
who take refuge in Him.
Psalm 18:30

More Jelly Beans, Please

Mark had cleaned his plate and was entitled to a treat. I grabbed a handful of jelly beans from a big pound-size bag and presented them to him. He gladly received the offered candy with an outstretched hand and began munching away.

Watching Mark eat the candy whetted my appetite, so I asked him for a couple. As he considered the request, I wondered if he would share with me. After all, I was the one who gave him the jelly beans initially. Would he give some back? I could get more from the kitchen to replenish his supply. On the other hand, he probably felt secure with the ones he already had.

Mark meandered over and gave me two of his precious jelly beans. That was difficult for him. He had candy, a scarcity for him, and he shared it with me.

Reflecting on this episode with Mark helped me see how blind I can be at times. God has blessed our family a great deal. And yet, when my husband receives his paycheck and he shares it with me, I sometimes hesitate to share it with God. His pay is barely enough to cover our monthly expenses. And unforeseen emergencies swallow up the rest. After comparing myself to Mark, I have to ask, "Why shouldn't I give back to God? After all, He gave it to me in the first place. And He is quite capable of giving me more if I need it. He even gave His Son to die on the cross for me."

Just like Mark, there seems to be security in what I hold in my hand. There is more security, though, in trusting someone who loves me unconditionally and is committed totally to taking care of me.

Dear Father,

Sometimes I forget how powerful You are and how much You love me and want to take care of me. Please help me to see all that You have provided for me. Enable me to give myself and my resources back to You cheerfully. Amen.

Now He who supplies seed to the sower and bread for food will also supply and increase your store of seed and will enlarge the harvest of your righteousness. You will be made rich in every way so that you can be generous on every occasion, and through us your generosity will result in thanksgiving to God.
2 Corinthians 9:10–11

Prayer Casserole

Nicholas crawled into the kitchen, whining for my attention while I sliced potatoes for the casserole. As I cut the ham, his whimpers turned to fussing. He settled at my feet to be near me. I stumbled over him as I moved to the stove to prepare the sauce. Then he wailed and clung to my leg as I "stirred constantly over low heat." I glanced down to see the shiny, wet face of my 10-month-old baby.

"Mommy has to get this in the oven, and then I can play with you. Crying isn't going to help." But the ache in my heart when I see my child unhappy overcomes my desire to get the job done the easy way. So I turned up the heat and picked up Nicholas so he could watch Mommy "stir constantly over medium to high heat." I finished the casserole with a consoled baby on my hip; I was free to play for a while.

Nicholas taught me a lesson. I picked him up because he had communicated that desire to me. One of the few ways for him to communicate at this point is crying. Just as it's important for Nicholas to communicate with me, it's important for me to communicate my needs and desires to God. That means taking the time to pray.

Nicholas did not whine once and then crawl off complaining. He kept crying, getting louder and more insistent. In 1 Thessalonians 5:17, Paul says to "pray continually." So keep on praying! And when Nicholas cried, he expected me to respond. Matthew 7:7 says, "Ask and it will be given to you." Pray, expecting God to hear!

God gave me prayer as a means of communicating. I can literally cry out to my heavenly Father. He hears my prayers, and He responds.

Dear Father,

Help me to communicate with You regularly and trust that You will hear and respond to me. Amen.

And will not God bring about justice for His chosen ones, who cry out to Him day and night? Will He keep putting them off?
Luke 18:7

"Markese"

My husband, Steve, claims to speak two languages: English and Markese. At times, Mark seems to speak a different language. Words like "goovee," "tobetty," and "goof driver" sound nothing like English. But his father and I understand most of what he is trying to say. I enjoy hearing 3-year-old Mark talk. I want to know what he is thinking about, what is important to him, and what he needs. At times, he sits on my lap and recounts in great detail his adventures. I treasure these times.

God treasures the times He spends with His children. He is *omniscient*—He knows everything that goes on in my life and in my head. So if I pray and tell God I had a lousy day, list everything that went wrong, and tell Him how I felt about it, He already knows. Yet He still wants to hear. He wants to hear how excited I am when I'm happy. And He understands me when I make no sense at all. He is with me through thick and thin. He knows the issues I am dealing with, my background, and why I handle things the way I do.

Just as I know that "goovee" means excuse me, "tobetty" translates to spaghetti, and "goof driver" is screw driver, God knows all about me and all my nuances. God wants me to talk to Him even though He already knows what I have to say. And He understands me even when I am unclear.

Dear God,

Because of Jesus, my Savior, I can come to You and talk to You as my heavenly Father. I want to climb up in Your lap and feel Your arms holding me close. I want to tell You what is in my heart and be understood. Thank You for always being there for me. Amen.

And pray in the Spirit on all occasions with all kinds of prayers and requests. With this in mind, be alert and always keep on praying for all the saints.
Ephesians 6:18

Baby Steps

"Come here, Nicholas," I called. "Come to Mommy." Nicholas took one hand off the couch and reached for me. He wobbled a little and grabbed the couch again with both hands. "You can do it," I encouraged. I was seated on the floor just a few feet from where Nicholas clung to the couch. He inched along the couch a little more and then looked for me. He was even farther away.

"Come here, Sweetie. Reach your hand for me." I stretched my hand toward him and when he reached for me, our fingers were only inches apart.

"You can do it. Come on." Nicholas slid his foot toward me and then fell into my arms.

"Yea! You did it! You took a step. Did you see that, everyone? Nicholas took a step!" Nicholas grinned as I paraded around the room with him in my arms. "Let's try it again," I said as I stood him by the couch and called to him again.

God calls to me. He calls me to repentance. He calls me to faith in Jesus. He calls me to live as His child each day, in every way. When God calls me to do something new, it is scary at first. I might fall or get hurt. But God would not call me without also supporting me. I may have to take baby steps at first. My efforts may not seem successful in the beginning. But if God calls me, He will be right there to help me and encourage me. If I fall, He will catch me or pick me up and get me started again.

Nicholas wobbled while taking those first steps. We kept working, and he grew steadier and more confident. Now Nicholas runs, kicks balls, dances, and jumps off the couch, all on his own two feet.

It can be frightening to take a step in a new direction, but with God's guidance and blessing, I can go places that I had never imagined before. I can trust God to lead me.

Dear Father,

Help me trust You and reach for Your hand. With You guiding me, I know I will be able to go far. Amen.

Teach me to do Your will, for You are my God; may Your good Spirit lead me on level ground.
Psalm 143:10

Me Want to Talk

Mark, Gramma is on the telephone. She wants to talk to you."

"Hi, Gamma, me won come over you's house. Me got new airplane and it flies real high. Me went on train ride and me not won get off but Mommy says we go home. Ummm, Nick-i-las taking nap-nap, bye." Mark handed me the phone.

"Mark, did you let Gramma talk? She wants to say something to you."

"No, me alweady talked."

That he did. He already talked, but he did not listen. Gramma wanted to invite him to the frozen yogurt shop, but he did not give her a chance to talk. This is a typical telephone conversation for Mark. He gets on the phone and talks until he has nothing left to say, and then he says good-bye.

This is a typical conversation for me too. When I talk to God, I start out with "Dear God." Then I tell Him what I need, sometimes I confess my sins, and then I try to remember to offer Him praise and thanks. When I am done, I say "amen" and go on with my life. I do not pause long enough for an answer.

In learning to listen for God to speak, I have found that He speaks in many different ways. He speaks to me through the stillness of my quiet times, through other people, and especially through His Word. All I need to do is listen. I have to be careful to make sure I do not answer for Him. (Sometimes I think I know what is best, but this may not be God's answer.) If I pray in the name of Jesus and leave myself open to His will, I am confident in His answer, whether it is "Yes" or "No" or "I have a better idea."

Talking to God is good. But I have come to realize that prayer life includes listening to God too.

Dear Father,
I am listening ...

My dear brothers, take note of this: Everyone should be quick to listen, slow to speak and slow to become angry.
James 1:19

I Love You

I picked Nicholas up from his crib and hugged him close to me. As I kissed his cheek, I said, "I love you." He snuggled up to me, resting his head on my shoulder so I would hold him until he woke up fully. He does not understand the words, but he does know that Mommy will snuggle with him, feed him, play with him, and try to make him happy and comfortable. He does not understand the love I feel for him. How could he? He's only a year old.

Mark is older and wiser; he's 3 years old. When I take him onto my lap, cuddle with him, and tell him, "I love you," he responds differently. Mark looks in my eyes, places his small hands on my cheeks, and says, "I wuv you too." He knows how to make Mommy happy. But as wise as he is, he still does not realize how much I love him.

Motherhood has shown me a whole new dimension of love that I never realized before. I give so much of myself and expect very little in return. I also know that my children do not love me to the same degree that I love them. That is okay; it is part of the nature of parental love.

This selfless kind of love has given me a minute taste of the kind of love God has for me. In the same way my children cannot fully realize how much I love them and what my love for them is like, I cannot comprehend the magnitude of God's love for me. He loves me so much that He sent Jesus to die for me, a sinner, so that I could become His forgiven child. I know that I will never be able to return God's love equally. But that does not stop Him from loving me. His love is greater than that. His love is greater than I can ever imagine.

Dear Father,

I know You love me and always will. I cannot even begin to show my love equally. I love You. Help my love to grow. Amen.

This is love: not that we loved God, but that He loved us and sent His Son as an atoning sacrifice for our sins.
1 John 4:10

Hug Me

Nicholas toddled toward me, crying. He held his finger up to my mouth and presented it for me to kiss. Apparently he wanted Mommy to make his "boo-boo" better. Once I kissed his finger, he was off to play again.

Before long Nicholas was crying again. This time he and Mark had struggled over a toy. Mark got possession of the toy and bopped Nicholas over the head with it. Nicholas was not hurt physically; he was crying out of principle. While I quickly disciplined Mark, Nicholas made his way to me, crying again. I picked him up and hugged him. That was all he needed. He struggled to get down and was off to retrieve the toy. He needed me only to recognize his pain. Then he was fine.

There are times when Nicholas gets hurt more seriously. He usually does not have to find me; I am there before he starts to look. I pick him up and hold him until the pain subsides. Then he slides out of my arms and is on his way.

Nicholas has found he has someone to turn to when he hurts. He can come to me with the little "owies," and he knows I will also be there for the big bumps. I am there to comfort him.

I get hurt and need comfort too. I may have a little owie, like hearing an unkind word from someone.

Then I can run to God and know that I am loved. Or if I experience a big bump, a major setback, God is already there, picking me up and holding me with tender care until I am strong enough to move on. He has power over my problems and pain, sickness and sin, even over death. God is always there for me. I can't imagine not having God to turn to, especially during major catastrophes. It is reassuring to know that He is there for me when I need Him.

Dear Father,

I need Your reassurance, Your love, Your forgiveness, Your encouragement. Thank You for being there for me when I need You. Amen.

God is our refuge and strength, an ever present help in trouble.
Psalm 46:1

Why?

hy is there water in there?" Mark pointed to the water in the bottom of the shower. Mark and Gramma were looking at her new house, which was under construction.

"They are checking to make sure it doesn't leak," Gramma said.

"Why it leak?"

"It doesn't leak."

"Why?"

"There wouldn't be water in it if it leaked."

"Why?"

"The water would have all leaked out."

"Why?"

"Well, if the builder comes, we'll ask him."

Mark asks "Why?" repeatedly, but it is not always the most effective question. He wants to know more, but the background he has to draw upon does not prepare him to even ask the right questions. A better question might be, "What happens if it leaks?" or "Where would the water go if it leaked?" But "Why?" is the only question he knows that will help him explore the subject. I continue to attempt to answer his questions because I want him to learn, even though at times the questions are exasperating and difficult to answer.

I frequently ask God "Why?" I especially ask "Why?" in the darkness of death, loss, or catastrophe. I always figured there was a good answer and that I just could not see it. But now I am wondering if I may be asking the wrong question. My background regarding the ways of God is very limited. I want to know more, and I want answers. But maybe I am asking "Why?" about things that cannot be answered in that way.

Maybe when I ask "Why?" and cannot find an answer, I should explore other questions. "What does God want to accomplish here?" "How is God glorified in this situation?" "What can I learn from this experience?" "Who is in control?"

While I may continue to have questions, I know that ultimately God is the answer.

Dear Father,

I do not always understand Your ways. Please help me understand what I need to and trust You to take care of that which I do not need to understand. Amen.

Trust in the Lord with all your heart and
lean not on your own understanding.
Proverbs 3:5

Dizzywand

"M̲e won go to Dizzywand." Mark jumped on me, bowling me over. "Why? Do you even know what you do at Disneyland?" I doubted that my not yet 3-year-old son would find anything enjoyable there. "Me won GO."

Reasoning was impossible while his favorite characters danced around the TV screen and a yellow sun zipped all about, enticing him to come to Disneyland.

This is the child who watches "Beauty and the Beast" from the other room. The Beast scares him. He screams when they turn the lights out at the movie theater. He cries his way off the Ferris wheel after only half the ride. Now he wants to go to Disneyland. Why?

I have been to the Magic Kingdom. It is enchanting. Bears sing, dolls dance, and the impossible is almost believable. But to my little son, the whole place would seem to burst with wild and scary things. So we wait.

I love Mark, so I say no to Disneyland—for now. God also says no to me sometimes. When I have prayed for and haven't received things that I think would make me happy, it seems like God does not care about my happiness. But God *does* care. He knows more than I what would make me happy. Maybe, like Mark, I am not ready. Maybe God has something else in mind that would make me happier. Maybe what I am praying for would hurt me or lead me down a path I do not really need to travel. I cannot always see what lies ahead. And I do not always understand God's reasons for saying no.

Fortunately, God's understanding and care are great. Jesus' death on the cross did not make any sense to His friends at the time, but look what a beautiful gift God gave through His Son to them and to us. God understood what we needed (forgiveness and salvation) and gave us His very best (Jesus).

Dear Father,

Thank You for saying no when no is the answer I need. Thank You for saying yes, through Jesus. I may not always understand Your reasoning, but help me remember how much You always love me. Amen.

I do not want you to be unaware, brothers, that I planned many times to come to you (but have been prevented from doing so until now) in order that I might have a harvest among you, just as I have had among the other Gentiles.
Romans 1:13

No-No

I heard a *thud, thud, thud* and a scream. I ran and found Nicholas screaming, his finger stuck in the fan. Terror surged through my body as I quickly turned the fan off and pulled his finger out. I started breathing again when I saw his finger was still there. A trip to the doctor revealed that it was not broken. Most of the damage occurred when I unhooked his finger from the fan's protective grating. The finger was cut, but thankfully, there was no permanent damage.

When we bought the fan, I had checked and thought that a child could not get his fingers through the grating. We told the children to stay away from the fan, that it was a "no-no." But Nicholas wanted to investigate for himself. When I turned my back, he took advantage of the opportunity and found the one place where the wires were bent just enough to get his fingers in. The result was painful.

God has "no-nos" for me too. He tries to protect me and lead me to safe places. If there is danger, He warns me with a "No." When I sneak off and try things on my own or ignore His warnings, I usually end up getting hurt. Often I discover that the reason He said no was to avoid pain.

Nicholas avoids the fan now. He had to learn the hard way that Mommy and Daddy were saying no because the fan could hurt him. I hope that he will learn to trust us and know that the reason we say no is for his own good. Through this experience, I realize that God has my best interests in mind also. When He says no, it is for my benefit, and I can trust Him to know what's best. He shows me His great love through His ready forgiveness in Christ. He leads me with His great love to follow His will for my life.

Dear Father,

I know that sometimes I ignore Your warnings and get hurt because of it. Please forgive me. Help me listen to You and trust Your judgment. Amen.

Listen to advice and accept instruction, and
in the end you will be wise.
Proverbs 19:20

My Way—or His Way

ark came in and presented me with a straw. I took it and went back to reading the mail. Then out of the corner of my eye, I noticed he was about three feet away, waving his arms and legs. Wondering what he was doing, I looked up. He had his arm cocked and his hand positioned just behind his ear. I suddenly realized that we were playing baseball and I was the batter. Buried deep in his small hand was a tiny rubber ball that he was going to hurl at me from a very short distance, and I would have to attempt to hit it with a straw. I laughed when I realized the ridiculousness of the situation.

I laugh also when I think how ridiculous some of my antics must seem to God. I get an idea in my head and try to make it work. I may even ask God for help, but then I don't stop to listen for His answer or directions. I proceed to tell Him how to accomplish my objective. I get frustrated when things do not seem to go my way.

If Mark had told me he wanted to play baseball, I would have taken him outside with his plastic bat and ball, and we would have had a real ball game. But with a plastic straw and a little rubber ball, we had no chance of being successful.

When I try to set the boundaries and tell God how I want things done, I can make it into an almost impossible situation. But if I give God room and allow Him the opportunity to solve the problem in His way, I have a much greater chance of being successful. He works with me so that together we can accomplish the task. God seems to come up with ideas that I never would have thought of, and often they are much better than I had dreamed of. (Who would have thought a birth in a manger and a death on a cross would save us from sin and give us the promise of heaven?)

I just have to keep remembering *who* is in control.

Dear Father,

I like to take charge and direct the way things should go. Help me trust in You and rely on Your superior judgment and wisdom. Please be patient with me when I forget and try to do things my way. Thank You for showing me Your way through Jesus. Amen.

*"For My thoughts are not your thoughts,
neither are your ways My ways," declares
the Lord. "As the heavens are higher than
the earth, so are My ways higher than your
ways and My thoughts than your thoughts."
Isaiah 55:8–9*

Busy, Busy, Busy

Nicholas filled a bucket with puzzle pieces and emptied it again piece by piece. Next he danced to the music from his tape player. For adventure, he climbed on the couch to look at the world from a different perspective. He had no wish to wait around to have his diaper changed. As soon as I positioned him on a clean diaper, he arched his back and scooted forward, twisting and reaching for a toy. He broke away and crawled off, only to be brought back again. All this fighting did not accomplish much. He was too busy to stop and wait for the diaper change, but his struggles only detained him longer.

I, too, am a busy person. I run around, seeing my own importance, too often leaving God out of my daily plans. God presents His will for my life, but I struggle against it. I fight and twist, reaching for other things, but He brings me back. I need to let God and His Word set my purpose even when it seems bothersome, time-consuming, or painful. When I submit to God and let His will be done, my life has direction and meaning.

This analogy only goes so far. It may be work, but I always get Nicholas diapered. God, however, does not force His will on me—not because He does not love me but because He gives me that option. He continues to call to me through His Word—

calling me to faith, repentance, and life in Christ, my Savior.

Dear Father,

I have been caught up in my own agenda and have not always given You the opportunity to work in my life. Please help me wait for You to work through me. Please fill me with Your love, in Christ, so that Your will also becomes my will for my life. Amen.

Do everything without complaining or argu-
ing, so that you may become blameless and
pure, children of God without fault in a
crooked and depraved generation, in which
you shine like stars in the universe.
Philippians 2:14–15

Tug-of-War

Mark meandered through the living room. His beloved blankie trailed behind him like a bridal train. The blankie caught on a toy that he had left lying on the floor. He kept going. When he had taken up all the slack, the toy held fast, and he stopped short. He tugged, but the blankie would not follow. Then he pulled and screamed in frustration. He accomplished nothing, so he cried for Mommy to come fix the problem. I directed him backward, unhooked the blankie, and sent him on his way.

Recently, I got hung up, and like Mark, I could not see the problem. I was trying to be a good mother. In my mind, that included denying my needs so that I could first tend to the needs of my family. I was rarely away from my children. I grew more tired and impatient each day. I was not the loving mother I wanted to be. When I finally cried to God for help, I felt He directed me backwards! He sent me away for a weekend retreat with my church peers. (I had originally wanted to go on this retreat but had said no because I felt my children needed me.) God showed me that everyone would be better off if I got some rest and returned to my family refreshed and with renewed patience.

When I have a destination in mind, I charge ahead. Going back seems counterproductive. If I am stuck, I would rather stand there and scream; it seems like a better use of my time. I usually cannot see the solution because I refuse to consider options that seem in opposition to *my* goal. But when I cry for help, God comes to my rescue. He turns me around and restarts me in the right direction, forgiving me through Christ and strengthening me through the Holy Spirit and His Word.

Dear Father,

Help me trust Your vision. Enable me to allow You to unhook me and turn me in the right direction when I cannot see what is wrong. Amen.

Do not conform any longer to the pattern of this world, but be transformed by the renewing of your mind. Then you will be able to test and approve what God's will is—His good, pleasing and perfect will.
Romans 12:2

Cleanup Time

Mark stretched his arms over his head as I pulled off his shirt. "Me not won baff." As soon as the shirt was off, he tried to run. I caught him around the waist and started removing his pants before he could take one more step. "I know, Sweetie, but I need to clean you up."

"Me not won kean."

"You have to take a bath anyway." I picked him up and set him in the tub. I tried to suds and rinse him quickly so that he could get out of the tub, but his protests and struggles slowed me down.

Finally, I grabbed a towel. "You can get out now."

"Me not won get out." I closed my eyes and exhaled audibly. "Me won play." Mark took his boat and dipped it under the surface, filling the hull with water.

I sat down on the floor and watched him play. I thought, Why did we have to struggle in the first place? His attitude made the bathing process miserable when the whole time could have been enjoyable.

My attitude, too, influences how well things go for me or what kind of struggles I have. When I find myself in an unpleasant situation, I have a tendency to grumble, complain, and focus on all the negative aspects. I even turn to God and ask, "Why did this have to happen? Why do I have to endure this?" I call attention to how unfortunate my circumstances are and try to make people feel sorry for me. And I end up feeling pretty lousy.

My other choice is to look for the positive aspects of my circumstances. I can begin by thinking about all that God has done for me. A positive look at my blessings leads to a positive reaction—a positive attitude.

Think about and thank God for the people in your life. Thank Him especially for His presence in your life, through Christ, your Savior, Lord, and Friend. If I can remember this, I might be more likely to try and find something good, even in giving reluctant children a bath.

Dear Father,

You have given me beautiful things to enjoy and amazing gifts of grace. Thank You. Please help me focus on these lovely and wonderful gifts rather than on the things that would destroy both the beauty and my mood. Amen.

Finally, brothers, whatever is true, whatever is noble, whatever is right, whatever is pure, whatever is lovely, whatever is admirable—if anything is excellent or praiseworthy—think about such things.
Philippians 4:8

The ER

ommy, help! Help me, Mommy! No, no, no, no, Mommeeeeeee!" The screams reached my ears from down the hall. My heart pounded. My stomach knotted. My mouth felt parched. I knew how scared Mark was, but all I could do was pace back and forth in the waiting room.

I was filled with a variety of emotions. My mind raced. *Would Mark lose his vision? I should have checked the house better. I should have checked on Mark again. Why weren't those chemicals locked up? My sweet little boy, my baby. He does not understand what they are doing to him. His eye is probably burning, and these strangers are pouring water in his face. He has to be terrified. I wish I could be in there with him to comfort him. He probably thinks I abandoned him.*

I tried to remain calm, knowing I wouldn't be allowed to stay with him if I became hysterical. I did my best, but the nurse decided I should wait outside. I think it was the shriek in my voice when I said, "You're putting him in a straight jacket?" So I suffered in the waiting room while Mark suffered in the examining room.

Sometimes it seems like God is removed from my pain, that He is not there when I need Him. But as I listened to my son's screams, I realized that God *was* with me. He suffered with me when I hurt. Just because He does not do something to stop the pain does not mean He is absent. I could have marched into the examining room and made the nurses stop hurting my son, but that action was not in Mark's best interest. So I endured the anguish with him. God endures a great deal of pain with me, too, rather than intervening. He knows what is best for me. His love and care is so great that He sent His Son to endure the pain of the cross for me.

Dear Father,

Sometimes I get angry because I think You do not care about what I am going through. Thank You for showing me that You do care and that You are always with me. Amen.

Be strong and courageous. Do not be afraid or terrified because of them, for the Lord your God goes with you; He will never leave you nor forsake you.
Deuteronomy 31:6

Where Are We Going?

ext week, we are going to move to our new house. Then we will set up the swing set Gramma and Grampa gave you for Christmas. And we will bring your train stuff." I was trying to prepare Mark for our upcoming move.

"And blankies?" Mark wanted to make sure he could take his beloved blanket.

"Yes, and blankies. We will also bring your tricycle, our clothes, and the couches."

"How?" he asked. His tone suggested that I was talking about impossible things.

Then I could see the picture that was probably running through his little head—Daddy trying to shove the big couch into the trunk of our mid-size car. Maybe Mark thought we would put the couch in the backseat along with Nicholas and himself, and he did not want a couch on his lap.

I smiled and said, "We have friends who will bring their trucks. Then we can put all of our stuff on the trucks and move it to our new house."

"Oh," he said.

Moving seems like such a major undertaking for Mark. I have tried to make it easy on him by showing him where we are moving and by explaining what is going to happen. But he is venturing into unfamiliar territory, and some of the things we are proposing seem impossible. After all, he only has limited experiences with the things of this world. He doesn't have years of knowledge to draw on to understand "moving."

When I venture into unfamiliar territory, I get a little edgy too. I like to know where I am going and how I will get there. But I have learned that I can proceed with confidence because God is always with me. When I envision a couch on my lap, I panic. With my limited experience and resources, I have no idea how to proceed. But then God delivers the answer when I need it, and in a way that I had not expected. He does this because of His great love. He graciously forgives me, strengthens me, and prepares the way for me to go. Then He guides me on my way.

Dear Father,

I have enjoyed seeing You work in my life. Help me trust You and rejoice in Your power and wisdom. Amen.

But if it were I, I would appeal to God; I would lay my cause before Him. He performs wonders that cannot be fathomed, miracles that cannot be counted.
Job 5:8–9

Playing Pretend

"Me kitty cat, now," Mark said as he dropped to his hands and knees, meowing. Then he crawled up onto the couch, placing each paw with great care. When he reached a high enough vantage point he pursed his lips, held his head high, and turned to survey the room with an air of sophistication that only a cat can possess.

Satisfied that all was in order, he moved on to the next matter. "Kitty wons milk ... on plate." I indulged my son and poured a little milk in a saucer.

As he lapped up his milk, I felt good that his body was getting some milk. I do not mind playing along with him when he pretends. It pleases him, and a lot of times playing pretend makes him more cooperative, like when I call him by his pretend name or let him lap his milk like a kitten.

I may play along with Mark, but I always know who he really is. I know Mark better than anyone else. And I believe I love him more than anyone else. I love him if he is a kitty cat, Peter Pan, or just plain Mark.

God knows me better than anyone else knows me. I am not fooling Him when I put on airs and try to be someone or something that I am not. He sees through the masks, the facades, right down into my heart. He sees my weakness and my sin and forgives me because of Jesus. God loves me because He made me. He loves *me*—as His dear child. It is a wonderful feeling knowing that I am loved "just because." God's love for me is not contingent on anything I have accomplished. God loves me when I am being sophisticated, motherly, or knowledgeable, or when I feel stripped of all worth. God loves just plain me.

Dear Father,

You see through all my outward appearances.
You see who I am—Your child. You even see
the parts I want to keep hidden, and still You
love me. You have shown Your great love
through Jesus, my Savior. You are so great and
Your love for me makes me worthwhile too.
Amen.

*O Lord, You have searched me and You
know me. You know when I sit and when I
rise; You perceive my thoughts from afar.
You discern my going out and my lying
down; You are familiar with all my ways.*
Psalm 139:1–3

Trekkies

ace ... final ear ... tarship Entepize ... Chssssssssssh!" Mark knows parts of the prologue to "Star Trek: The Next Generation," ending with the starship accelerating into warp drive.

"Shuuuu," Nicholas stands right in front of the TV for a good view and then mimics the spaceship taking off. He hunches over, his arms extended behind him and runs through the house saying, "Shuuuu." Mark and Nicholas are able to perform these little scenes because they are exposed to them so often. Daddy watches Star Trek almost every night. These episodes have become a part of who the boys are.

I ask myself, "What am I exposing myself to so often that it is becoming a part of me?" I enjoy watching movies, but they do not always match my personal value system. Yet I find myself drawn into the characters' lives and values. I enjoy the movies but run the risk of incorporating Hollywood values into my life.

God has given me the Bible to use as a guide for my life. And I have read God's Word to me. But I do not like reruns, so why would I want to read the Bible again? Advertisers have the answer in our everyday lives. They know what benefit it is for me to hear the same message over and over. Through their repeated message, they make their product a part of my life.

Mark has not only learned the prologue to Star Trek, but he also knows bits of several commercials. He has learned them through constant exposure. God knows that if I am constantly exposed to Bible verses and passages, His Word will become a part of who I am and will be there for me to draw on when I need it. God's important message comes to me through His Word and His Sacraments. His good news that Jesus has died for my sins affects my life now and eternally.

Dear Father,

You have given me Your Word to help me with my daily life. You have given me Your Word to tell me of Jesus, my Savior. Help me hear and learn it. Help me trust Your promises of forgiveness and life eternal. Amen.

All Scripture is God-breathed and is useful for teaching, rebuking, correcting and training in righteousness, so that the man of God may be thoroughly equipped for every good work.
2 Timothy 3:16–17

Swimmer

ool!" Nicholas seemed to say as he made a beeline for Grampa's pool. Nicholas was too little to talk, but the determination in his eyes declared what he was thinking. Nicholas was also too little to swim, but that did not stop him. He tore right up to the edge, turned around, and scooted backwards, reaching with his feet until he slid over the edge of the pool. He depended on Mommy to catch him. Then we splashed around enjoying the cool break from the heat.

We enjoyed playing in the water, but Nicholas' charge to the water scared me. He had no regard for the danger the pool presented. With this in mind, I was almost glad when Nicholas slipped under the water for a second before I could catch him. The water invaded his nose and filled his mouth. As I grabbed him and held him close, he wrapped his tiny arms around my neck and clutched me until he quit spluttering. Then he rested his dripping head against my shoulder and clung to me like a wet leaf.

I want to protect Nicholas from everything that could hurt him. But sometimes letting him learn firsthand what he is jumping into is more protection than trying to rescue him. Nicholas has more respect for the pool now. He still scrambles in any chance he gets, but he eases himself onto the step and then looks for me. He is also learning how to swim.

God sometimes allows me to slip and fall. I may charge ahead, trying to do things my way without realizing the dangers or my own limitations. When I fall it seems devastating, but God does not leave me to face trouble alone. He calls me to cling all the more tightly to Him. Instead of drowning in my own ignorance, God calls me to rejoice in the victory He gives me through His Son.

Dear Father,

Catch me when I jump and when I fall. I need You to hold me and protect me. Sometimes I do not always see the danger; thank You for opening my eyes. Amen.

Show me Your ways, O Lord, teach me Your paths; guide me in Your truth and teach me, for You are God my Savior, and my hope is in You all day long.
Psalm 25:4–5

Natural Consequences

lifted Mark onto my lap to visit with him. We had had a couple of difficult days. Mark was being rebellious. He wanted to see just how much he could get away with and what Mommy would do to enforce the rules. Mark is still quite young and is learning what behavior is acceptable and what is not. These stretches in which he requires constant discipline and correction strain me. Even though I am worn down, I welcome the opportunities to spend treasured time with Mark. I thought this was one of those rare moments as he snuggled into my arms and we talked about playing in the nursery at church. Then, without warning, he reached up and swatted my face.

"You must not hit Mommy. If you hit again, I will have to put you down." He looked me in the eye and swatted me again. I sighed as I kept my word and put him down. I do not think Mark fully realized what he lost in the exchange.

On another day, we planned a trip to the park. Mark resisted getting dressed with every ounce of energy he had. Since Mark refused to get dressed, we stayed home. Our change of plans was a natural consequence rather than a punishment. We could not go to the park if he was naked.

As I strove to create opportunities of positive interaction with my son, I realized that maybe I make it hard for God to give me blessings. I have a rebellious streak. Maybe God was longing for the opportunity to love me and to give me His gifts, but I was fighting against Him. Maybe I was getting in the way of receiving His blessings.

At times when things were not going well, I wondered if God was punishing me for something I had done wrong. Now it does not seem so much a punishment as a natural consequence of living in this sin-filled world. For I have come to know that God's love is great and that He always stands ready to forgive. He has made me His child through salvation in Christ Jesus. And He is eager and able to turn my life around, making me a new person—His forgiven and blessed child.

Dear Father,

Please forgive me for being rebellious and for fighting You. Thank You for loving me, even through my rebellion, and for not giving up on me. Thank You for Your forgiveness for Jesus' sake. Amen.

Yet the Lord longs to be gracious to you;
He rises to show you compassion. For the
Lord is a God of justice. Blessed are all
who wait for Him!
Isaiah 30:18

My Brother's Eye

Mark pushes his brother, Nicholas, and tears the ballpoint pen out of his hand. "You not s'posed to have this." Mark is right of course, but now I have a baby screaming because he was pushed down and deprived of his toy. Mark does not consider that his own actions are inappropriate. He feels it is necessary to right all wrongs, especially when it comes to his brother. I send Mark to his chair for a time-out, but Nicholas goes undisciplined. When Mark intervenes like this, it becomes difficult for me to instruct properly. My reprimand would be lost in Nicholas' wails.

I often fall into the same trap as Mark. I have a tendency to condemn others who are not living by God's standards. I criticize someone for his or her action, but I am guilty of the same "crime" or a worse one.

My husband has felt the brunt of my judgment more than anyone else. At first, I thought it was my duty as a wife to make him perfect. I told him when he said the wrong things, wore the wrong clothes, and engaged in the wrong activities. At least they were wrong according to me. But I was not getting through to him. All I did was make him angry.

When I finally gave up, an interesting thing happened. He started asking my opinion. Before, there had been such commotion between my complaints and his defenses that God's message to us in His

Word was lost in the ruckus. But when I was quiet, God could be heard.

When Mark tries to discipline his brother, maybe even using the same techniques that I would, he aggravates the situation. When I want to discipline my husband—my Christian "brother"—I aggravate the situation.

It is still hard for me to remember that God is so much better at handling corrections than I am. But now when I want to correct others or make them perfect, I remind myself to mind my own affairs and allow God to handle the disciplining of His children. I remind myself that we are made perfect only through the forgiveness and righteousness of our Savior, Christ Jesus.

Dear Father,

Please forgive me. I am a sinner, and I have hurt You and my brothers and sisters in Christ. Please forgive me for passing judgment on others when I am guilty too. Amen.

Do not judge, or you too will be judged. For in the same way you judge others, you will be judged, and with the measure you use, it will be measured to you.
Matthew 7:1–2

Whose House Is It Anyway?

"**C**ome back and wipe your feet! You are tracking mud into the house." In my mind, I saw footprints across the like-new, cream-colored carpet. "Absolutely, positively NO food or drinks in the living room." Again, visions of a stained carpet sprang to mind.

"Don't drag that stick against the wall. You are going to tear the wallpaper." The little bit of wallpaper the previous owners had used was tasteful and added just the right amount of color to our new home. I knew that it would be quite some time before I would have the time, energy, or money to redecorate, so I was hoping to keep everything looking good.

"Don't kick your feet against the wall! You are leaving black marks." The people who previously owned this house did not have children. They had left it in excellent condition. I had been so excited to find such a nice house that fit into our budget. But I was beginning to wonder how long this nice-looking house would last.

I collapsed in the only kitchen chair we had brought to the new house. Mark, Nicholas, and I had come to do a little cleaning before everything was moved in this weekend. I was beginning to think that the boys would tear it down before we could move in. I wanted my children to enjoy our new home, but not to the point of destruction. We all have to live here.

God gave me a larger home that I share with millions of other people. In the beginning, God created a magnificent world for my home. Through the years, it has shown the wear and tear of misuse, destruction, and disregard. God redecorates with each new season. But some of the destruction is permanent and ongoing.

I imagine it upsets God when He sees me treating the earthly home He gave me with a lack of respect. Though I do not live here alone, I do need to consider how I can honor God by caring for the home He gave me. I want to do what I can to preserve the beauty. I go to God for help: "Forgive my mistakes. Empower my actions."

Dear Father,

So often I do not even think twice about the beautiful home You have provided for me. Thank You for the beauty and the continuous restoration that You provide. Help me do what I can to preserve the beautiful gift You have given me. Amen.

The earth is the Lord's, and everything in it, the world, and all who live in it; for He founded it upon the seas and established it upon the waters.
Psalm 24:1–2

A Gift for You

ust before Mark's third birthday, we browsed through the toy store, looking for ideas. It was there that Mark spotted a pull-toy helicopter that he wanted. From that point on he followed me around the store telling me of his great need, "Me want hel-i-caco. Me show you. Come wif me, Mommy." What impressed me most was that he never lost control. He never resorted to whining. He did not throw a temper tantrum. But with his birthday coming soon, he did not need another toy. So Mark did not get anything that night.

When we got home, I suggested we count the money in his piggy bank. His life savings totaled $7.03. He was short about a dollar. I then gave him the option of doing chores to earn money. He worked hard. He got a nickel for taking the aluminum cans out to the recycling box, a dime for helping me sort laundry, and a quarter for helping pick up toys that were scattered all over the house. When he finally had eight dollars plus enough change for tax, we went back to the toy store and purchased the helicopter. Mark was proud of his hard-earned toy.

Though he had earned this toy, it had really come from me. By paying him for doing chores that I had created, I gave him the means to earn the money.

Just as Mark's toys are gifts from me, my hard-earned accomplishments are really gifts from God. He has given me my abilities and the opportunities to use these talents. He has provided these gifts, and my working for them makes me more appreciative and responsible.

Even with help, Mark cannot earn everything he needs. His dad and I provide the necessities and more. God provides many things for me, too, the most important of which is my salvation. Try as I might, I cannot earn it. But God has given it to me, through His Son, Jesus, who died on the cross to save me from sin. Through this sacrifice, I have the promise of heaven. That is God's best gift to me!

Dear Father,

Thank You for Your many gifts, both the ones I have to work for and the ones You give me outright. Thank You especially for giving me eternal life with You through the saving action of Your Son, Jesus. Amen.

For it is by grace you have been saved, through faith—and this not from yourselves, it is the gift of God—not by works, so that no one can boast.
Ephesians 2:8-9

Unconditional Love

 came home from the store and dangled the sack that held my purchases in front of Mark. "Look what Mommy bought today," I sang. "What is it?" Mark reached for the bag. He seemed to be able to tell by the tone of my voice that it was something good.

I began pulling out items and listing them as I displayed them. "Paint. Paint brushes. Sidewalk chalk. And just for you ... a brand-new box of crayons."

Mark seemed frozen as he saw all the goodies that I had brought for him. Then just above a whisper he said, "Thank you." Then in the sweetest voice he said, "I love you, Mommy."

I love him too. But my love is not dependent on a box of crayons or even whether he tells me he loves me. It makes me feel good to hear him say he loves me, but I love him *always.*

Only a few days later, his tune changed. He emerged from his bedroom after a time-out and declared in a loud defiant voice, "I don't like you anymore. I only like Daddy. You go to work and Daddy can stay home with us."

Though his words stung, my love for him remained the same. I loved him just as much as when I had bought him the crayons. His love may be fickle, but my love for him is not dependent on how he feels about me.

God's love for me is constant also. Whether I am good or bad, praising Him or throwing a temper tantrum because I did not get my way, He loves me. His love is always there, no matter how I feel toward Him. And He loves me whether He is bestowing blessings on me or disciplining me.

What a comfort to know that God's love for me is not dependent on how I behave or even how I feel toward Him. God loves me not because of who I am but because of who He is—He is good. He is forgiving. He is love.

Dear Father,

Thank You for Your constant and unconditional love. Amen.

But God demonstrates His own love for us
in this: While we were still sinners,
Christ died for us.
Romans 5:8

Gimme, Gimme

unt Kim had presents for all the kids at the family reunion. Both of the 3-year-olds, Mark and his cousin Camren, got a big box of cars. They were delighted. We quickly marked each car so there would be no confusion as to which one belonged to whom. Both boys began playing with their new treasures.

Soon after, I heard screaming and unintelligible threats coming from the living room. A red-faced Mark sat hoarding all 24 of his cars in a bucket, protected within his legs. He was screaming at Camren who was playing with one car on the floor nearby. Mark wanted *that* car. But on closer inspection, we discovered that car belonged to neither one of the boys but to *Grandma*. It was community property.

I was dismayed. Mark had been given a very nice gift. He received more cars than he could play with at one time. But he could not enjoy any of them because he was so consumed with the desire for more.

My chagrin was compounded when I realized that I can be very much like Mark. God has blessed me so richly. Not only does God meet all of my needs, but He also provides me with quite a few luxuries. Still I want more. I get my mind set on something I want and forget about everything I have. It is okay to want things; God even tells me to make my wishes known to Him. But when that desire for more is a driving force in my life, I have gone too far. If I stop and look at the "24 cars" God has already given me, I cannot help but feel thankful.

Dear Father,

Please forgive me for Jesus' sake. When my greed for more has clouded my vision, and I have forgotten all that You have given me, help me to be thankful for all that I have instead of complaining about what I do not have. Thank You for Jesus, Your best gift of all! Amen.

*Keep your lives free from the love of money
and be content with what you have,
because God has said, "Never will I leave
you; never will I forsake you."
Hebrews 13:5*

Little Helper

Nicholas ran into the garage to help. He was excited about getting to ride in *his* car. But it was not easy to get the vehicle out. This giant, colorful plastic toy was almost as tall as my waist and wide enough for Nicholas and three of his favorite stuffed animals to sit in comfortably. Besides that, I had to try to maneuver the coupe around Mark's tricycle and between boxes that were stacked in the garage. So Nicholas decided to help. He had his hand firmly fixed to the door frame and no amount of persuading could convince him that I could manage a lot quicker on my own. The look of purpose on his face let me know that he believed his role was important. So I let him help.

I pushed the car slowly so I would not run over Nicholas. He was in front pulling as I pushed from behind. Even though I tried to compensate for the tug on one side of the car, we still ran into the lawn mower. When I tried to renegotiate the passage, Nicholas pulled harder on his end. He did not want to go backwards. It was slow going, but we finally got the car out. Nicholas played for quite a while in his car.

I try to help God sometimes too. I may give God suggestions on how things should be done, or I might take matters into my own hands. I have even felt like God was going the wrong direction and tried to correct the problem. It never occurred to me that I might be getting in the way.

When I am trying to help God, maybe He is saying to me, "Let Me handle this. It would be more helpful if you did what I asked in the first place." But even if I get in the way, God still gets His objectives accomplished. He just works around me. I would be more helpful to God if I did what He wanted me to do instead of trying to take charge and make Him follow my orders. Praise God that He forgives me through Jesus and that through the Holy Spirit, He empowers me to live a new life for Him.

Dear Father,

I want to be helpful, but sometimes I get carried away and get in the way. Help me remember who is in charge and to do what You want me to do. Amen.

I have considered my ways
and have turned my steps to Your statutes.
I will hasten and not delay
to obey Your commands.
Psalm 119:59-60

In the Spotlight

T he church was decorated for Christmas, and the excitement mounted as the Sunday school got ready for the children's Christmas service. The music started, and I escorted the 4-year-olds down the aisle to a pew at the front of the church. I dragged Mark behind me. He should have been with the 3-year-olds, but he had refused and insisted on staying with me. He had been disagreeable all morning.

When we reached the pew, he threw a tantrum because he did not want to sit in our assigned spot. I picked him up and sat him on my lap and he calmed down. When we went in front to sing, he decided to scream rather than sing. When he finally settled down, he continued pulling on me while I tried to lead the 4-year-olds. When we returned to the pew, he threw another tantrum; I wanted to hide.

As I sat crying silently in church, I felt as if every pair of eyes in the entire congregation was looking at me, judging me to be a terrible mother. I felt if I had handled things better before we got to this point, Mark's tantrum and my feelings of frustration would not have happened. Maybe I should not have even expected Mark to participate. I felt as if his actions reflected my parenting skills. I wondered if all the other parents were having second thoughts about leaving their children with me for Sunday school. I was ashamed because of my son's actions.

Later that afternoon, I thought about the situation in a different context. I thought about times when I have embarrassed God. I make no secret about the fact that I am one of God's children. But when I sin, I bring shame and great disappointment to my heavenly Father. God bears the humiliation of these indiscretions. And yet, my Father still loves me. The love of Jesus is quite evident; He took on all my shame—past, present, and future—and died for my sins. And the power of the Holy Spirit helps me to grow in my life as God's child.

Dear Father,

I know at times I have acted in ways that are shameful. Thank You so much for loving me anyway. Thank You for Your willingness to forgive me for Jesus' sake. Amen.

You are the light of the world. A city on a hill cannot be hidden. Neither do people light a lamp and put it under a bowl. Instead they put it on its stand, and it gives light to everyone in the house. In the same way, let your light shine before men, that they may see your good deeds and praise your Father in heaven.
Matthew 5:14–16

Art Gallery

ark bounced up to me after nursery school was over. He handed me his latest master-piece—a turkey. He had painted his hand, pressed it on to the paper, and then drew the face and feet. He loves to paint and is always thrilled to present me with a new creation. It is fun for me to receive these child-made gifts.

I took the turkey home and put it on the refrigerator beside Mark's finger-painted cloud and the pumpkin with three eyes and a crooked smile. After an appropriate showing time, I put his creations in my "save box" to pull out later and admire. They also document his development. These projects may not be art to anyone else, but to me they are valuable possessions because I love Mark.

As I admired the "Mark Collection" with all of its "imperfections," I thought about my very real flaws. I am a perfectionist and quick to notice my own inadequacies. I know that when I stand before God and offer my best work to Him, it always falls short of His standards. But at the same time it probably pleases Him because He loves me and enjoys watching me grow.

This Christmas, our family is sending Christmas cards that feature Mark's art on the front. The prayer inside refers to a child's heart, so on the outside, I wanted a heart colored by a child. Mark's imperfect scribbles add charm to our special greeting card.

God uses my imperfections too. My strengths are important, but so are my weaknesses. Weaknesses make me more approachable, more sympathetic, and more understanding of my friends who struggle with some of these same weaknesses. God turns my weaknesses into strengths because He is able to work through my weaknesses. He is greater than my strongest strength.

Dear Father,

Help me realize that when I am not perfect,
You still can use me to accomplish great things.
I praise You that the perfect heart I lack and
need is now mine through the forgiving love of
Jesus. Amen.

*But He said to me, "My grace is sufficient
for you, for My power is made perfect in
weakness." Therefore I will boast all the
more gladly about my weaknesses, so that
Christ's power may rest on me. That is
why, for Christ's sake, I delight in weaknesses, in insults, in hardships, in perse-
cutions, in difficulties. For when I am
weak, then I am strong.*
2 Corinthians 12:9–10

God's Child

efore Mark and Nicholas were born, I longed for a child. I tried every way to get pregnant—various medical procedures, going to chiropractors, and standing on my head. But it seemed like I would never have children. So when I finally conceived, I excitedly announced the news to everyone from my great-aunt Margaret to my co-workers at school. By the end of the second month, I was buying baby furniture, setting up the nursery, and studying the book of baby names.

When I miscarried the baby a week later, I was devastated. Though that child had been ours for just a short time, it was still our child, and I mourned our loss.

Six months later, I sat in church on Christmas Eve, knowing that I was losing another child. I begged God to let me keep this baby. I tried to turn the situation over to Him; I tried to trust God to handle it in the way He saw best. But I was angry. I did not want to lose this baby too. I wanted a baby, but there was nothing I could do to save this child.

I sat in church and tried to worship. I tried to celebrate the birth of Jesus, knowing there would be no birth in our near future. As I thought about these two babies—the one I would never hold in my arms and the one God sent to save the world—I began to consider what Jesus' birth must have meant to God. We were celebrating Jesus coming to earth. Coming to earth to be born, to live, and then to die. To die so that my sins might be paid for. God gave up His Son. God sacrificed Jesus for me. Willingly.

For as long as I can remember, I have known that God gave His Son to die for me. But it was not until I knew what losing a child was like that I could better grasp the magnitude of God's gift.

God really does love me.

Dear Father,

Thank You for Your love and thank You for the gift of Your Son. Amen.

For God so loved the world that He gave His one and only Son, that whoever believes in Him shall not perish but have eternal life.
John 3:16

Praise Him

My friend Tennie was seated in the passenger seat of my car as we drove to one of our favorite stores. Tennie stopped talking mid-sentence. Then almost from nowhere, she said, "Rebecca likes me more than a horse with wings."

I laughed and asked, "How do you know?"

"She wrote it on one of her papers last year when she was in kindergarten."

I glanced over at her. There was a faraway look in her eyes as she stared out the window, almost as if she were transported to another time and place. Her smile grew as she recounted all the details for me.

I know how she felt. My children have yet to be so eloquent, but they have shown and told me of their love. If I go out for a little while, my return is celebrated with shouts of, "Mommy's home!" Then I am nearly bowled over by little bodies flinging themselves at me.

Mark loves to bring me flowers. He will run back and forth to the yard, presenting me with an entire bouquet, one weed at a time. Those weeds are more beautiful to me than a dozen long-stemmed roses. I do not think that there are many things that make a sweeter sound than when Nicholas sits on my lap and tells me, "I luff you, Mommy."

Moments like these can lift my spirits and make me feel whole again. And as evidenced by Tennie, these times of praise have the power to continue uplifting us. As meaningful as these times are, we don't do things to earn this praise. Tennie and I both do the things we do based on our love and commitment to our children, not because they say we are wonderful.

God's love for me is not dependent on my praise of Him; it is not dependent on *anything*. But as much as God has done for me and as much as He loves me, isn't He deserving of my praise?

Dear Father,

I do not even know how and where to begin to offer praise to You. You are so great and so good! There is nothing that I could compare You to, not even a horse with wings. I love You. Amen.

Praise the Lord, all you nations; extol Him, all you peoples. For great is His love toward us, and the faithfulness of the Lord endures forever. Praise the Lord.
Psalm 117:1-2

Long Sleeves and Long Pants

ark came into the kitchen holding the clothes that he had picked out to wear for that day. I took one look at them and said, "No, you can't wear those today."

"I want to wear these." He started taking the clothes off the hanger.

"It is too cold. You have to wear long sleeves and long pants. You've been wanting to wear your new sweats; why don't you wear them?"

"I want to wear shorts."

"It's too cold." The weather had just changed, and I had not had an opportunity to move the summer clothes out of his closet. He probably thought his mother was pretty fickle. Just over a week ago I insisted that he wear shorts when he wanted to wear sweats. Now I insisted on the reverse.

I strive to be consistent. I may not always succeed, but I am a lot more constant than Mark thinks. Naturally, as a 3-year-old, he just does not always take into account the external circumstances that influence my decisions. I tried to explain the weather to him, but some things do not seem to matter to a 3-year-old.

God is consistent. There is no "striving to be." He is. And like Mark, I may not always understand how

God will handle a situation, not because He is unstable but because He knows everything and takes into account all the circumstances. I have no way of knowing what influences God's decision in each situation, but I can take comfort in the fact that He makes the best decision for my present life. And because of the saving grace of Jesus, He will give me an even better life in heaven—a perfect life with Him.

Dear Father,

Again, I do not understand Your ways. Nor do I understand on what You base Your decisions. What I do know is that You love me and You are unchanging in that love. I depend on You. Amen.

Jesus Christ is the same yesterday and today and forever.
Hebrews 13:8

Hide and Seek

Me want to eat this." Mark waved a piece of candy in the air. "You need to wait until after dinner," I said. "Weave." He glared at me with a defiant look. He seemed to think that if I were not in the room, I would not know that he was disobeying me.

I did not leave. I just smiled at him.

"Me gonna hide." I wanted to laugh, but I refrained. Mark thought that he might be able to hide and get away with it. He made his intentions clear and then thought I might not know what he was up to. As far as his hiding goes, I have seen him hide before. A child-sized lump bulging from the middle of a blanket thrown on the floor gives away a hiding preschool child very quickly. Mark really cannot hide from me.

There have been times that I have tried to hide from God. If there is something in my life that is less than honorable, I think if I ignore it, no one will notice it, not even God. I have also tried to hide from God by ignoring Him. I turn my attention to other things and turn my back on God. I think maybe He won't notice what is going on in my life. I even try to bury my sins in excuses. I think the more reasons I can come up with to justify my actions, the less noticeable the sin is.

I may not have been ducking behind a chair or trying to leave the room, but by hiding, ignoring, or excusing my sins, I was hoping that God would not see what was going on. I was trying to cover my weaknesses. But God always sees me. Sometimes I do not realize how transparent I am to Him. He knows what my intentions are. He sees the defiance in my heart and mind and my attempts to hide. And He calls to me. Through His Word, He calls me to repent and to receive forgiveness through the cross of Christ.

Dear Father,

You know I am not perfect and I make mistakes. I only compound my problems when I try to hide from You. I know that if I go to You, You will help me deal with whatever it is I am struggling with. But to be honest, sometimes I do not want help. I want to be able to do whatever I want. Help me remember how much You love me for Jesus' sake and that You want me to have joy, not just for a moment, but forever. Amen.

Where can I go from Your Spirit? Where can I flee from Your presence? If I go up to the heavens, You are there; if I make my bed in the depths, You are there. If I rise on the wings of the dawn, if I settle on the far side of the sea, even there Your hand will guide me, Your right hand will hold me fast.
Psalm 139:7–10

I Sawwy

Mark watched as I took my contact lenses out for the day. I poured the cleaning solution into the little vial, then proceeded to remove the first lens. As soon as I had the lens in the palm of my hand and cleaner all over both hands, Mark picked up the vial and started playing with it.

"Don't touch, Mark." I scrambled to free my hands. "Put that down." Mark ignored me and kept playing with the vial. He spilled the solution all over the counter and in the sink. I sighed. I did not say anything as I refilled the vial, placed it out of his reach, and deposited the contact lens.

"I sawwy, Mommy."

I turned and looked at him. His brown eyes seemed bigger than usual as he looked up at me. The smile that had been on his face when he was fiddling with the vial was gone. Even though I had not said anything after he dumped the solution, he knew that he had disobeyed me.

I reached down and squeezed him next to my leg. "It's okay, Sweetie." How could I be angry when he said he was sorry? He rarely says he is sorry. I had not even asked for him to apologize. He did that from his heart.

"The sacrifices of God are a broken spirit; a broken and contrite heart, O God, You will not despise."

These words from Psalm 51:17 always seemed a little intimidating to me. It seemed like I would only be pleasing to God if I were battered and beaten.

I am the first person to want Mark to be self-confident. But when I saw his broken and contrite heart, I was pleased. His repentance showed me that his sense of responsibility had developed to consider others ahead of himself. He showed me that he loved me enough to feel remorse for his inappropriate actions.

The broken and contrite heart that pleases God is in a person who cares beyond herself or himself and feels remorse when his or her actions hurt God or others. Just as I want my child to care about others and feel a responsibility for his behavior, God also wants me to feel remorse and admit my sins. Then He announces to me through His Word and Sacrament the forgiveness and transformation found only in Christ.

Dear Father,

Please forgive me for the times that I do not obey and for the times I just do not think. I am sorry. Help me change my ways and turn to You for help and guidance. Amen.

Create in me a pure heart, O God, and renew
a steadfast spirit within me.
Psalm 51:10

The Big Lie

was spooning macaroni and cheese onto plates when I heard the bathroom door slam, followed by Nicholas' wails. I dropped the spoon into the pan and stormed down the hall. How many times have I told that boy not to slam the door to stop his brother?

When I reached the bathroom, I found Nicholas in the hallway, still crying, and Mark close by, looking smug.

"What happened?" I demanded as I picked up Nicholas.

Mark said, "Nicholas hurt himself."

"When you slammed the door?" I asked.

Mark shook his head, "No, Nicholas hurt himself." He looked at the door.

I looked into his eyes. "Are you lying to me?" I asked accusingly. "You will be in more trouble for lying than for doing something wrong."

Mark shook his head; the tears welled up in his eyes. I could feel my muscles tightening. He was lying to me again. Then the shake of his head slowly turned to a very slight nod.

"You did close the door on Nicholas!"

Mark nodded again with tears in his eyes. Then the tears filled my eyes too. I reached over and hugged him. I was shaking inside.

"I should punish you because you lied. But since you just told Mommy the truth, I will let it go this time."

Mark nodded again. He had been upset by the whole matter. It was hard for him to admit that he had done something wrong. Then when he lied about it, he was in an even bigger mess. He looked relieved when it was all over.

It is hard for me to admit when I am wrong too. I try to bury my wrongdoing, forget about it, pretend that it did not happen. I do not want to face my sin. But when I go to Jesus, my Lord and Savior, and tell Him the truth, He gives me His gracious love and forgiveness. It does not make what I did less wrong, and I may still have to endure the consequences, but I can go before my Lord with confidence. I can tell Him that I'm sorry and trust that He will forgive me and always welcome me into His arms.

Dear Father,

It is so comforting to know that no matter what I do, I can rely on the loving forgiveness You so readily supply through Jesus, my Savior. Thank You for Your grace and mercy. Amen.

The Lord is compassionate and gracious,
slow to anger, abounding in love.
He will not always accuse,
nor will He harbor His anger forever;
He does not treat us as our sins deserve
or repay us according to our iniquities.
Psalm 103:8–10

The Robot

 sat in the middle of the living-room floor, cutting up a box as Nicholas ran circles around me with a big grin on his face. He stopped and shouted, "Wo-bot!" I had found a box that would work perfectly as the square body for the robot costume Nicholas wanted me to make. I figured a few holes for arms and head, an aluminum foil covering and a foil-covered hat would make a perfect robot costume.

"Nicholas, come here. Let's try this on you and see how it fits."

He came running over, and I started to slide the box over his head, but the box was rigid and did not conform to his body. I was having a little trouble getting his arms through the armholes. I fidgeted with the box, trying to align it so that his arms would slide in. Nicholas stood in the middle of the room with his arms straight up and a big box covering his face. It was dark, and he could not see inside the box. "Off! Off! Off!" he cried as he wriggled to get free.

"Nicholas, Mommy almost had it. Let's try again. I will work faster this time."

"No."

I sighed. Did he think I would hurt him? Doesn't he know how much I love him? I wouldn't do anything to hurt him. Doesn't he trust me?

Another thought struck me. I do not always trust

God. I feel as though I don't know what is happening or that this is different than what I am used to. Or like Nicholas, I may not be able to see, and so I get scared. But why don't I trust God? Don't I know how much He loves me?

God has shown me again and again that He is trustworthy and that He takes care of me. But when I am faced with a new situation, I have a tendency to doubt because I cannot see what God is doing. God's Word reminds me that He alone can help me by forgiving my weakness and strengthening my trust in Him. Maybe now I will have the courage to close my eyes and wait as God "slips the box" over my head so that I can move on in my new costume.

Dear Father,

You have always taken care of me. You have always done what is in my best interest. By the power of the Holy Spirit, help me remember Your loving care when times get scary and I start to doubt. Focus me on how much You love me through Jesus. Amen.

Jesus replied, "I tell you the truth, if you have faith and do not doubt, not only can you do what was done to the fig tree, but also you can say to this mountain, 'Go throw yourself into the sea' and it will be done. If you believe, you will receive whatever you ask for in prayer."
Matthew 21:21–22

Priorities

have to clean this kitchen, I thought to myself. I've let it slide because I've been busy with other things. They were important things, and I wouldn't change anything I did, but now the kitchen has priority. Nicholas was playing with a toy in the living room; Mark was coloring at the kitchen table. I figured if I moved quickly, I could whip the kitchen into shape in no time.

As I scraped the gook off of last night's dinner dishes, Mark asked "Mommy, how do you make a 'M'?"

I froze for a moment. Then I put down the half-scraped plate and went to sit by Mark at the table. "You want to make an 'M,' Sweetie?"

"Like my name." His big brown eyes stared up at me, waiting for me to show him how to make the letter.

I smiled at him as I picked up a crayon. I made an "M," and then he made one. Then we worked on his whole name. The cluttered kitchen did not matter anymore. The dishes could pile to the ceiling; I'd get to them later. Mark wanted to learn how to print his name and now that was our priority. I make myself available when Mark wants to learn.

I could not help thinking about how God responds when I ask Him to teach me. When I am asking to learn, when I am seeking wisdom, He is there, by my side, showing me the things He wants me to see and teaching me the things He wants me to know. I can ask at any time and trust that He is ready to answer.

As I think about my experiences with God, I am amazed at the times I have asked for wisdom and that is exactly what He has given me. It makes me wonder, Why don't I ask more often?

Dear Father,

I ask You for wisdom in all I do and say. But most important, I ask You to help me to be wise enough to remember to ask You to teach me. Amen.

If any of you lacks wisdom, he should ask God, who gives generously to all without finding fault, and it will be given to him.
James 1:5

Beauty

icholas gasped as his mouth dropped opened. When he turned to look at me, there was a shine in his eyes. "Baby." He smiled and turned his attention back to the baby who had just joined our table.

The eating part of the church dinner was over, and the softball awards ceremony was about to begin. People were milling about and socializing with friends at other tables. Baby Emily and her family had come to visit our table.

"Baby," Nicholas said to Daddy, in case he had missed the new arrival.

"You can go see the baby if you want." Nicholas slid off my lap and started around the table. "Baby," he said to each person he passed on his trip around the table.

Nicholas stopped directly in front of the baby. Emily, seated on her mother's lap, reached for Nicholas. As Emily's hands got nearer, he remained still, held his head steady and closed his eyes. Nicholas allowed her to feel his face. Then she reeled backwards with a squeal and Nicholas opened his eyes and grinned. The two repeated this routine several times. The smile never left Nicholas' face.

A smile never left my face either. I thought Nicholas was the sweetest thing in the world at that moment. His face shined with beauty as he smiled at Emily.

In my attempts to be beautiful, I spend a great deal of time in the bathroom fixing my face, hair, and clothes. But this is not where true beauty lies. God tells me that beauty comes from a gentle and quiet spirit. Beauty comes from *within*.

I could see this beauty clearly in my son. Though his baseball outfit made him look cute, his gentle spirit delighted everyone at the table. Perhaps my "beautifying time" would best be spent not in front of the bathroom mirror but rather in the Word of God, listening to His gentle and quiet voice of love for me, His forgiven child.

Dear Father,

Sometimes I get too caught up in outer beauty and worry about how I appear to others. Give me Your Spirit. Help me learn the gentleness that You value. Thank You for making me beautiful in Your sight. Amen.

Your beauty should not come from outward adornment. ... Instead it should be that of your inner self, the unfading beauty of a gentle and quiet spirit which is of great worth in God's sight.
1 Peter 3:3–4

Brotherhood of the Blankie

icholas fell, bouncing his forehead on the kitchen floor. I scooped up a screaming, kicking little boy. Hugging Nicholas close to me, I kissed his forehead. A lump emerged, but he had not broken the skin. Before I could calm Nicholas, Mark was beside me holding Nicholas' blankie up for me to take. I smiled at Mark as I took the blanket. Nicholas rested his head on my blanket-clad shoulder and quieted down. I sat in the rocking chair with Nicholas while Mark went back to playing. Mark knows the value of the blankie more than I do. He has one of his own. And if Mark gets hurt, Nicholas is the first to find Mark's blankie for him.

This brotherhood of the blankie goes beyond injuries. If Mark is in a time-out, he knows that I will not bring him his blankie. He asks Nicholas to get it, and Nicholas does. If someone's blankie has to be washed, that is a call for real sympathy. The boys have even offered me their blankies when I was sad or hurting. I appreciated the gesture, but I really have no use for a ragged, grungy blanket.

But, like the boys, I do have need for comfort and encouragement. God, in His love, has provided people with whom I have a kinship through similar circumstances, experiences, or dreams. These "brothers" and "sisters" understand my needs because they may have experienced the same feelings. I, in turn, can be a source of comfort to a friend because I may have been in a comparable situation. And we can share with one another the comfort of the almighty God who cares for us with an unconditional love.

I believe this is one of the real values of fellowship with other Christians and of being a member of a church body. It is in this Christian fellowship that God connects us with our brothers and sisters in Christ. The best blanket of encouragement that we can offer each other is based in the Word of God.

Dear Father,

Thank You for providing Christian "brothers" and "sisters" to walk with me and lift me up. Help me to be a source of strength to others, too, by telling them of the comfort and peace found only in You. Amen.

And let us consider how we may spur
one another on toward love and good deeds.
Let us not give up meeting together,
as some are in the habit of doing,
but let us encourage one another—
and all the more as you
see the Day approaching.
Hebrews 10:24–25

Attitude Adjustment

Mark half-walked, half-skipped across the parking lot to the bank. Both boys look forward to these trips since we switched to a bank that offers cookies to the customers. As soon as we were inside the door, Mark dropped my hand and dashed for the plate of cookies.

"Take just one," I said as he reached for the plate.

He grabbed two cookies.

"I said one." So he offered one of the cookies to his brother.

Nicholas cried, "I want other one." Since Mark had chosen not to listen to me and touched two cookies, I allowed Nicholas to have his choice. Mark refused to accept the other cookie, and I completed my transactions amid his wails and demands.

Mark's attitude at the bank was not a singular event. That same day he ordered me to carry his blanket and book in from the car. Just as he did not get the cookie, I did not carry his valuables. I love my son and want to do things for him and give things to him, but I am not going to let him think it is okay to make demands or scream if he does not get his way.

God cares about my attitude too. He does not want me to make demands and place my will above His. When I was in the midst of my second miscarriage, I gave the situation over to God except for one little detail. I felt that since I had been so "noble" as to relinquish control to God, I could justifiably ask one favor of Him. I asked God not to let me lose the baby on Christmas Eve or on Christmas Day. I did not realize it at the time, but I felt God owed me something. So when my demand went unfulfilled, my anger burned, and I felt betrayed by God.

The whole idea of humbling myself before God seems to take on a new light now. God is not asking me to belittle myself but to come before Him with an attitude of respect, an attitude of humility.

Dear Father,

Please forgive me for the times when I have the attitude that You owe me something. Remind me that You love me with an awesome attitude in Your perfect love, and You forgive me for Jesus' sake. Help me remember that it is I who owe my whole life and everything in it to You. Amen.

Humble yourselves, therefore,
under God's mighty hand, that He may lift
you up in due time.
1 Peter 5:6

Train Layout

The first thing we saw when we entered Grandma's house was Camren, my boys' cousin, sitting on the floor playing with his wooden train set. Immediately, Mark and Nicholas wanted to play with their train set too. So the three boys set to work constructing a larger design. Camren had enough track to make a figure eight; but when all the pieces were combined, the boys could make an elaborate layout with two hills and multiple lines.

The harmony lasted for about a day-and-a-half. Then screaming brought me to the living room. Camren and Mark were each clutching a train on the track while trying to remove the other's train with his free hand. It was a head-on collision and each 3-year-old wanted his own right-of-way. Trying to rationalize with them did not work. Camren started pulling apart the track that Mark had built. "I want an eight!" he screamed.

"No!" Mark answered at full volume. "I don't want an eight."

"Okay," I said. "We'll divide the track and you can each play with your own pieces." I quickly sorted the track by the markings we had placed on them.

This ended the screaming, but it also ended the fun. There were now two boxes with track pieces and train cars. Camren did not get his "eight" because he did not know how to put it together. Mark was not worried about a structured layout, but he was reduced to only one hill and no caboose.

God tells me in His Word that in giving and sharing I will be blessed and receive more. I could see this clearly in the boys' play. Separately, they had a functional train set, but together they could stretch an elaborate set-up across the living room.

I sometimes hesitate to share because it seems that once I do, I will not have control of that particular item anymore. But when I have shared, it always seems as if I have more and receive many blessings from sharing. I've learned this from the one who has taught me all things in His Word, the one who changes my heart through His forgiving and transforming power. That one is Jesus, my Lord and Savior.

Dear Father,

Thank You for the great wealth You have given me. Help me appreciate the treasures You have given me, and help me share them with others. Amen.

One man gives freely, yet gains even more;
another withholds unduly, but comes to poverty.
A generous man will prosper; he who refreshes
others will himself be refreshed.
Proverbs 11:24–25

Ready or Not

e need go pee-peeeee!" Nicholas wailed as he clutched himself. "Well, hurry up. Go in the bathroom." He was just beginning his potty-training, and sometimes he waited too long. Nicholas stood in the living room and pulled his pants and underpants down to his ankles. Then he walked like a penguin toward the bathroom.

"Nicholas, if you wait until you get to the bathroom to pull your pants down, it will be much easier." I scooped him up and quickly carried him the rest of the way to the bathroom, just in time.

Nicholas had the right idea; his timing was just a bit off. He was learning the steps, but he did not have them all quite in order. I can relate to this. I have a tendency to get ahead of myself at times too.

I start worrying about things that are down the road a ways. I look ahead and see where I want to be and then start thinking and acting like I am already there. Planning ahead is fine, but when these preparations get in the way of reaching the ultimate goal, I bind myself at the ankles, and it slows my progress.

God has a way of getting accomplished *what* He wants *when* He wants. I can make all the preparations I want, but if it is not His time, then I will not get very far. On the other hand, if He wants something done immediately, He can do that too. Even if, like Nicholas, I have created a hindrance for myself, God can zoom me to where He wants me to be.

When I give my plans to God, He sees to it that things get done when they need to—in His time and in His way. I do not have to worry about the things to come. He will work them out or help me to deal with them when the time is right.

God's plan and His timing are perfect. He demonstrated this when He sent Jesus to be born and to die for our sins. In His perfect timing, Jesus conquered sin and death.

Dear Father,

You know how anxious I get to have things done NOW. I get carried away and start making preparations when my time would be better spent on other things. Help me trust Your timing. Amen.

He has made everything
beautiful in its time.
Ecclesiastes 3:11

Tunnel Vision

I discreetly slipped into the pew between my husband and my friend Amy. I had just returned from my crouched-down position in front of the church. I had moved to a good vantage point to snap a picture of Mark in the Sunday school Christmas program.

Amy leaned over and whispered, "Did you see Ryan? He didn't sing anything. His little sister knew the songs better than he did."

Ryan? I thought as I smiled at Amy. I didn't even notice Ryan. In fact, I can't remember what any of the other children did or said. I felt embarrassed. Here I was sitting with my friend, and I had not even taken the time to glance at her son.

I don't think I even took my eyes off Mark. I am sure that Mark did not captivate the rest of the audience. He looked stressed. His mouth moved, but it seemed to be an effort for him to do the motions. More often, he tugged at his cheek or twisted his hands together. He smiled one time, when he saw me crouched down in the aisle with my camera ready.

No, he definitely did not have stage presence. But that did not matter to me. He was the one that I wanted to see because he was my son. I delighted in seeing him participate in the special service. I noticed all the flaws, but I love him so much that none of that mattered. I was smitten and not because of any redeeming traits on Mark's part.

When I stand before God, He focuses on me. None of my flaws are hidden from Him. He sees them all just as if a stage light were illuminating them. And yet He loves me. It is not because of any redeeming traits on my part. He loves me because I am His own child through Jesus' saving work.

Dear Father,

You know me inside and out. You know me better than I know myself. Though I do not like to have my faults on display, it is wonderful to know that You love me anyway. Amen.

For the Lord is good and His love
endures forever; His faithfulness continues
through all generations.
Psalm 100:5

But ... I Want It

Mark shook one of his Christmas presents and then brought it into the kitchen. "These are my Ninja weapons, aren't they?"

Oh, no! I thought. He is going to be disappointed. "Mark, come here." I pulled him close. "You are not getting Ninja weapons. I did not get you any, and I don't think anyone else is going to get you any either."

Mark ripped away from me and screamed, "I told you I want Ninja weapons; you wrote it on my list."

I had asked Mark to list some things he wanted for Christmas. He studied catalogs and sale flyers and came up with two pages of the things he wanted most. The Ninja weapons were not an oversight. I did not feel it was an appropriate gift for a 4-year-old. There were so many other things that I felt he would benefit from and enjoy.

"Sweetie, I can't get you everything on your list. But I think you will like what I did get you."

"I want Ninja weapons." His face contorted into a grimace as he started crying.

I was upset at first. I really wanted him to be happy and enjoy the Christmas activities. But then I got angry. I had gone to a lot of trouble finding gifts that would delight him. There were things from his list as well as other items that I thought he would enjoy, even though they were not on his list. His father had spent hours building and painting a puppet theater, while I put curtains on it and found puppets to use with it. I thought of the puppy we had arranged to pick up on Christmas Eve. I felt indignant that Mark would be so demanding, but I reminded myself that he was young and just learning about giving and receiving.

Just like I asked Mark to make a Christmas list, God tells me to make my requests known to Him. But that does not mean I have a magic lamp to get whatever I want. When I make my requests known to God, I may feel that I must get one certain thing or I will never be happy. But God may choose *not* to give that to me. He may surprise me with something that is not even on my "list."

Dear Father,

You know what is best for me, what I need and what will delight me. Forgive my demands and impatience for "my answer." Thank You for giving me things that I never even dreamed of along with all that I really need. I especially thank You for Your gift of Jesus, my Savior and friend. Amen.

For the Lord God is a sun and shield;
the Lord bestows favor and honor;
no good thing does He withhold from
those whose walk is blameless.
Psalm 84:11

The Great Puppy Defense

I heard some kind of noise and rolled over, hoping that it would go away. The noise continued, and I awoke enough to realize that Nicholas was crying. I climbed out of bed and stumbled into the boys' bedroom. When I first looked at Nicholas' bed, all I saw was a puppy dog tail wagging back and forth. Then I saw the puppy attached to the tail wiggling just as fast, all over Nicholas.

"Noel," I said as I lifted the puppy off Nicholas, "he was sleeping." I knelt beside Nicholas and tried to comfort him. The new puppy did not sleep through the night. Every night she would wake up and want someone to play with her. She usually chose Nicholas because his bed was the only one low enough for her to jump on.

"Sleep yours bed?" Nicholas asked, still crying.

"Sure." I carried him back to bed and glanced at the clock. Three in the morning. I groaned to myself. "We've got to do something about that dog," I mumbled to my husband as I settled back into bed.

We came up with a great solution. We found the baby gate that had not been used in ages and put that up. Now Noel could not get into the boys' room, and Nicholas was not terrorized anymore, at least not while he was sleeping.

Our wonderful solution had a problem though. While Noel could not get in, neither could the boys get out. They were safe, but they were prisoners in their own bedroom. They were not free to come and go as they chose. They could not crawl in bed with Mommy and Daddy unassisted.

The barriers that I create to protect myself from something or someone can be just as binding as the gate we put in the boys' room. When I put up a wall to protect myself, I also limit my freedom. God wants me to build on my relationships rather than build up walls that hinder relationships. Without a wall to protect me, I may feel vulnerable, but that vulnerability will be the first step in rebuilding a broken relationship.

By erecting barriers, I imprison myself. These self-imposed barriers limit my access to everything, including God. Sin once separated us from God. But Jesus has broken down that barrier, reconciling us to God. And He empowers us to build relationships with others based on His forgiveness and love that fill our hearts.

Dear Father,

Some relationships seem impossible, and I would rather just walk away from them. Help me break down the barriers and find strengths in each relationship. Through the power of Your Spirit, rebuild and strengthen my relationship with Jesus and with others. Father, I know I cannot do this without You. I need Your freeing power and help. Amen.

Let us therefore make every effort to do what leads to peace and to mutual edification.
Romans 14:19

Your Side

 oth boys rode silently in their car seats in the backseat of the car as I approached the freeway. But just as I turned onto the ramp, I heard Nicholas order, "Your side!"

I did not know what he meant, but Mark did and replied, "The sun might get in my eyes, so I have to look out your window."

I laughed out loud. Since I was driving, I could not look back at Nicholas, but I could imagine his pressed-together lips, the stare in his eyes, and the indignant look on his chubby little face. His rights had been violated. Fortunately, he was appeased by Mark's response.

Later during the same trip, he again commanded, "Your side."

"I can look out any window I want," Mark answered.

I had heard this squabbling over the direction of a sibling's gaze, but this was the first time I had experienced it with my own children. It was hard to believe that they would argue over something so trivial. What harm was being done? What was the point?

"It's a matter of principle." This is usually my line of defense when I am questioned about my reason for getting involved in a trivial disagreement. There are principles that are worth defending. But there are also times when I let minor irritations become destructive agents within relationships.

I am learning that if I turn to God and give the whole situation to Him, He helps me see what is truly important. He forgives my misdirection through Christ and guides me in the right direction through His Word. By focusing on the Lord and what He wants for me and in my life, I do not get so caught up in the little things and can accomplish the important things.

Dear Father,

I need Your help in determining what is important and what I need to let go. Keep my eyes focused on You and Your will. Amen.

Do not seek revenge or bear a grudge against one of your people, but love your neighbor as yourself. I am the Lord.
Leviticus 19:18

The Road to Grandma's House

re we almost at Grandma's house?" Mark asked for the tenth time. I clenched my teeth and took a deep breath. I glanced at Steve and we exchanged a smile. "No, Sweetie, we still have quite a ways to go."

This satisfied Mark for a while. I glanced out at the Los Angeles traffic we were trapped in. Normally, we would have been there by now. We had the trip to the grandparents well-planned. We knew when to travel and when not to. We had studied the map and had backup routes in case of an accident. This day, though, it seemed as if there were accidents on every freeway in LA.

"When are we going to get there?" Mark asked again.

I looked at the sun starting to sink in the sky and glanced at my watch. "It will be dark when we get there." I hoped this would give Mark a frame of reference. I knew how hard it was for him to wait, especially when he could not see to the end. He just didn't have a concept of how long it would take.

I could sympathize with Mark. I get antsy when I am unsure of what is going on or when I will finally reach my goal. Even when I travel down a road I have been on before, different circumstances can change how it looks, what happens along the way, and even how long the trip takes.

It is especially unnerving when I can't see the end. I often think that I would feel better if I could see the whole picture and know exactly where I am going and where God is taking me. Giving Mark maps of LA and Orange County would not have helped at all; just knowing that we would get there after dark was the biggest help to him. Probably seeing the whole picture of what lies ahead in my life would not help me either. But God gives me daily indications and directions to help me along the way. And I am certain of my final destination. That certainty I have in Christ.

Dear Father,

I know that I constantly come to You questioning where we are going and how long it will take to get there. Help me rest assured that You have a plan. Give me comfort from the insights and direction You provide for me. Thank You for the sure direction and love You give me in Jesus, Your Son. Amen.

Show me Your ways, O Lord, teach me
Your paths; guide me in Your truth and
teach me, for You are God my Savior,
and my hope is in You all day long.
Psalm 25:4–5

Don't Worry

Mark, I want you to get down from there."
Mark balanced on the arm of the couch.
"You don't need to worry about me." He
jumped from one couch to the other, landing on one foot on his "balance beam."

"I don't?" I asked.

"I can take care of myself; I'm strong." He slid to the
end of the armrest and stood proudly, looking down
at me from his perch.

"Get down anyway."

This overconfidence in his own ability can change
without any notice.

"I need to go potty," Mark whined.

"Well, go," I said.

"Come with me." He shifted from side to side.

"Mark, you can go by yourself."

"No, I can't. Come with me."

"Why can't you go by yourself?"

"I'm afraid." He looked down the hall. "There might
be monsters."

"There are no monsters. I will be right here."

For me, I usually feel in control when things are

going well. I can take care of anything, and I don't need any help as long as there aren't any problems. But it's precisely at these moments that I am in the greatest danger of falling. I am overconfident and not paying attention to what God or anyone else might be telling me. But if I do fall, I'm sure I will want God to rescue me.

God's greatest act of rescuing was when He saved me from sin through Christ's death on the cross. Jesus forgives my moments of overconfidence and my moments of fear. He leads me to trust that He is always near.

Dear Father,

I do not always listen to You very carefully. I worry about things that You have told me not to worry about, and then I do not pay attention to times when You urge caution. Help me to listen to Your words and to trust You. Amen.

Do not think of yourself more highly than you ought, but rather think of yourself with sober judgment, in accordance with the measure of faith God has given you.
Romans 12:3

Learning the Hard Way

"**M**ark and Nicholas, it's time to settle down. You're getting too rough." The two boys laughed as Nicholas grabbed hold of Mark's legs and they both tumbled to the ground. Mark thrashed about until he was free. He jumped up and tore down the hallway.

"Mark, no running in the house. You are going to get hurt!" I called after him. Nicholas trailed right behind him. I followed the two boys, planning on taking hold of each one and sitting them down so they would settle down.

But before I got there, Mark made a U-turn and started back the same way he had come. Nicholas, still in hot pursuit, collided with Mark, and they both fell to the floor. Nicholas seemed to get the worst of it; at least he was screaming the loudest. I cradled Nicholas and rocked back and forth while Mark held his elbow out for me to kiss.

Mark's elbow and Nicholas' head hurt for a short time, but the boys finally calmed down. It took pain for them to finally listen.

We have rules in our house that are designed to keep us all safe, help us get things accomplished, and treat each other with respect and dignity. We do not have restrictions just for the fun of it. In fact, God's commandments serve the same purpose.

God may try to warn me when I am making poor choices. God may use a multitude of media to get His message across—His Word, other people, past experiences, my conscience. But so often it takes pain for me to get the point. Either I can listen to what God is telling me or I can choose not to listen and learn the hard way.

When it comes to obedience, I need help. And help is there in Jesus. He is ready to forgive our disobedience, and He is eager to empower us and to enable us to live in loving obedience as people of God. This can happen only through Him. And because of Him, it will happen. Jesus took our sins—our disobediences, pains, and sufferings—to His cross so that we might be forgiven.

Dear Father,

Sometimes I am so tempted not to listen and to ignore the rules. Please help me remember that You gave me the rules for my protection and because You love me. Lead me to live as Your child. Amen.

Listen to advice and accept instruction, and
in the end you will be wise.
Proverbs 19:20

It's Just Not Right

Nicholas' breath was awful. He was an adorable blond-headed, green-eyed, chubby-cheeked toddler with breath that could curl your hair. While I was in the bathroom getting ready to go shopping, I put toothpaste on his toothbrush and said, "Here, Nicholas, brush your teeth." Nicholas stuck the toothbrush in his mouth while I tried to finish applying my makeup.

"Nick is not brushing his teeth," Mark announced. "He's just sucking the toothpaste off the toothbrush."

"That's okay, Mark. He's still learning how to brush his teeth. He will get better with practice." Besides, all we really need is for his breath to smell a little better, I thought. I'll make sure the teeth get cleaned later.

"But he's not doing it right."

I realized, through this simple daily situation, that I need to think twice before telling someone that his or her way is wrong. Someone may not be doing things the way I would, but that does not make the other person's method wrong. I do not know how God is working in the lives of others, or how God may be using others to reach someone else.

Recently, my church put up a computerized electronic outdoor sign. When I saw the new sign, my initial reaction was, "How commercial. How tacky! I can't believe the church did this."

Soon after that, a friend told me, "Bob and I were driving by your church and were so thrilled to see the new sign. Our church in Texas used a sign like that, and they witnessed to many people."

I wasn't accustomed to the new sign, so I jumped to the conclusion that it must be wrong. I had not stopped to consider how it might touch someone's heart with God's message.

I have to admit now that the sign touches me too. I read it every time I pass by. I already have the information that it shares about services and activities, but a line from a familiar hymn also is displayed with every message. It only takes that one line to start me singing. A lot of times, the hymn's message stays with me the whole day.

God has His own ways. He can even work through a computerized sign.

Dear Father,

When I start to think something is wrong, help me look at it from another perspective. Help me remember that You use many different things to accomplish Your goals. You even gave Your only Son, Jesus, to accomplish Your goal—to save people from sin. And let me look for the value in things so I am not so quick to condemn. Amen.

Therefore judge nothing before the appointed time; wait till the Lord comes. He will bring to light what is hidden in darkness and will expose the motives of men's hearts. At that time each will receive his praise from God. 1 Corinthians 4:5

Letting It Heal

on't scratch that, Nicholas, you are making it worse." Nicholas turned his back to me and kept scratching. He had a patch of irritated, scaly skin that was itching and driving him crazy.

"Sweetie, I know it itches, but you are making it worse by scratching it." I moved toward him, but he ducked behind the chair to continue scratching. I retrieved him and sat him on my lap. "Look at this. It is bleeding where you scratched. I know it bothers you, but if you leave it alone, it will get better and then it won't hurt anymore. Let's put a bandage on it."

Nicholas had the bandage on for only a few minutes when he cried, "Bandage off. Hurt."

I checked the bandage to make sure it was not too tight. "We have to leave the bandage on so you don't scratch anymore. I will call the doctor first thing in the morning."

"Ringworm," the doctor said the next day. "Put this medicine on and it will help."

The medicine did help. The skin started to heal, and Nicholas got relief from the itching. But from time to time, I still caught Nicholas scratching. He would tear at the skin and make it bleed. The medicine continued to do its work even though Nicholas would open up the wound and slow down the healing.

It's hard for me to wait and allow time for my wounds and blemishes to heal. I can be just as tenacious at scratching as Nicholas, even when I know that I am making it worse. It seems like the scratching will give me some kind of relief. If I have done something wrong, I am highly critical of myself, and I will pick at my problem. When I pick at myself, I only irritate the affliction, making it worse rather than better.

Jesus, our Great Physician, gives us forgiveness and healing for our lifelong affliction of sin and its consequences in our lives. By the Spirit's power, He helps me to quit criticizing myself, to stop irritating my vulnerable spots. I need God's forgiveness at full strength. I need and I trust Him to heal me.

Dear Father,

Thank You for the forgiveness and the healing You give through Your Son, Jesus. Help me quit tearing myself apart. Heal me and help me accept myself as Your loved and forgiven child. Amen.

If we confess our sins, He is faithful and just
and will forgive us our sins and purify us
from all unrighteousness.
1 John 1:9

I Need ...

oppp! Go back." Nicholas called his directions from his seat in the shopping cart. I back-peddled a few steps to see what had caught his eye. "What did you see?"

"Sucker," Nicholas said grinning up at me. I smiled back at him and continued on my way.

"Toppp! Me need sucker."

I laughed, "No, you don't *need* a sucker. We have plenty of goodies at home."

"Me won," Nicholas whined.

"You may want it, but you definitely don't need it. There's a difference."

I'm sure Nicholas did not see much difference between wanting the sucker and needing it. At that moment, he probably could not even think of anything else. The line between want and need was too blurry for this toddler.

I could see more clearly; in fact, I could see a large chasm between want and need in this case.

God is willing to give me a lot of special treats too. He indulges me because He loves me. But as with Nicholas, my line between want and need gets blurry at times. Maybe that is because I am blessed with the reception of so many wants that I rarely have to face a true need. I forget how abundantly God has provided for me.

Recently, I thought I needed a new dress. But I had

trouble finding one. I told God of this "need." I think
He must have laughed as He helped me remember
the bags of clothing we give away each year. Then I
started to explain to God why I deserved a dress. But I
knew I did not "deserve" it. So I tried to rationalize, "It
would be so much easier to give my presentation at
the ladies' luncheon if I had a new dress." I finally
ended with, "I just want it."

I found a dress in my closet and decided that I could
wear it. Then the day before the luncheon, I found the
perfect dress on sale, which brought it within my budget. I did not *need* it, but God gave it to me anyway.

Nicholas needed my attention and love. He got it. I
needed to feel good in a new dress to do my best job.
However, most of all, we *need* Jesus' unconditional
love and gracious forgiveness each day. God provided
for our greatest need by sending Jesus to die on the
cross in our places. We do not deserve this gift, but
God knows how much we need Him!

Dear Father,

Thank You for all the frivolities that You shower
on me. Help me remember that they are special
treats from You and that You more than abundantly meet my needs. I praise and thank You
for Jesus and the salvation and forgiveness He
has won for me! Amen.

*Now to Him who is able to do immeasurably more than all
we ask or imagine, according to His power that is at work
within us, to Him be glory in the church and in Christ Jesus
throughout all generations, for ever and ever! Amen.*
Ephesians 3:20–21

Birthday Present

ithout saying a word, Nicholas came up to me and held up a toy police car for me to see. My first reaction was vague recognition. Then I thought, Does he have a police car like that? I don't remember giving him one. That's like the one we got for ...

Suddenly I realized what happened. "Nicholas! You weren't supposed to open Katie's present. That's for her birthday." I took the police car and marched into the living room where I had left the package. There on the floor was the rumpled wrapping paper and torn box.

"I want pees car," Nicholas said.

I put the police car back in the torn box and was about to punish Nicholas, but I remembered that it is not so easy for a toddler to give something good away. "Come here, Sweetie. I know you want a police car, but we got this for Katie."

"No. Nicky."

"We got it for Katie's birthday. She gave you a present when you had a birthday."

Nicholas thought about this for a moment. "Me won pees car."

"I know."

Nicholas was learning a lesson in giving. He had not been prepared for giving the gift away. Katie's birthday came right on the heels of Christmas, and

Nicholas was still accustomed to having presents come his way. This time, he had to take the gift and give it to his friend.

There are times that God gives me something for the sole purpose of giving it to someone else. He could give the gift directly to the person He had intended it for, but in giving it to me first and having me give it away, both the recipient and I benefit. I have the opportunity to give something to someone else *and* witness how my gift enriches the other person's life.

God the Holy Spirit helps us share the good news of Jesus' saving action on the cross with others. The Spirit helps us tell others of His best gift—the Savior— and the importance of sharing His gift with everyone.

Dear Father,

You have blessed me with so many gifts! You have even given me some gifts to share and to give away. Help me realize what others need and enable me to share with a loving and gen- erous heart. Most important, give me the words and actions to tell others about Jesus, my Savior—Your best gift to the world. Amen.

And God is able to make all grace
abound to you, so that in all things
at all times, having all that you need,
you will abound in every good work.
2 Corinthians 9:8

Because I Said So

ark and Nicholas, it's time for a bath." I started running water into the tub. Nicholas took off in the other direction. Mark asked, "Why do we have to take a bath?"

"You are both really dirty. You played in the sandbox and in the mud. It will feel so good to clean up."

"But we cleaned up when we came inside."

"You are still dirty. You need a good, *thorough* bath." I retrieved Nicholas and carried him to the bathroom, where I began undressing him.

Mark took his clothes off. "See, I'm not dirty. I don't need a bath."

"You ran around outside and got all sweaty. You were in the sand, the mud, and the grass. You *need* a bath."

"Why?"

"Because I said so."

It is important for my children to learn that they need to obey me just because I am their mother. I love them and I look out for their best interests. I cannot, and will not, stand in the middle of the street with a 2-year-old and explain why he cannot play there.

I think it is vital to treat a child with respect. When I explain my rationale sometimes, I'm showing respect. I also believe it is important for children to learn obedience. They need to learn to obey even when they don't have all the information.

God demands my obedience, whether I understand or not. He gives us His commandments to guide us in our everyday living. I think that if I knew what He was trying to accomplish, it would be easier. But I'm sinfully human and fail constantly on my own. Only by the power of the Spirit working in me am I able to acknowledge my disobedience and tell God I'm sorry. Then, for Jesus' sake, God forgives me and draws His child close to Himself, thoroughly cleansed by His gracious love.

Dear Father,

I want to obey You. I know that You love me and want only the best for me. When I disobey and fail, remind me that it is not a power struggle. Work in me the desire to love You even more, just as You already loved me with a boundless love. Thank You for Your constant love and forgiveness freely given for Jesus' sake. Amen.

But if anyone obeys His word, God's love is
truly made complete in him.
1 John 2:5

Stretching

wondered if I was doing the right thing as I reached for the Sunday school door and pulled it open. The last time I brought Mark to Sunday school, he could be heard screaming several classes away.

Since his promotion to the 4-year-old class, he fought against going and declared that he hated Sunday school. We had been through this before though. His resistance the previous year had diminished as soon as he had gotten to know Mrs. Dravis. She had provided activities with glue and paint, taught fun songs, and brought snacks and colorful stickers. Mark had known exactly what to expect.

Now I figured that once he got to know Miss Jan and her routine, he would want to go. So I persisted. I braced myself as I pulled the door open. Mark walked right in. He found his teacher and started toward her. Miss Jan hurried over to greet Mark the moment she saw him. "How was your trip to see your grandparents?"

I stood in shock as he told Miss Jan all about going to his grandparents and showed her the toys he had brought. When I kissed him good-bye, Mark assured me, "I'm gonna have fun." Then he was off to put a sticker on the attendance chart.

I sat in church that morning wondering what had happened. What—or who—had changed Mark's attitude? Maybe it was the postcard Miss Jan had sent that told

Mark she missed him and that she looked forward to seeing him when he got back from his grandparents. Maybe it was the sucker she had promised him at the end of the last class. Maybe he was beginning to realize that Miss Jan was pretty nice.

As the pastor began his sermon, I felt as if he were talking directly to me. He told us how God continues to allow us to experience uncomfortable situations. It's through these situations that we grow and stretch. Eventually what was unpleasant becomes more comfortable and sometimes is even a blessing.

I know that my sinful nature will continue to cause disquieting and awkward times—even times of frustration and utter despair. But because of God's continual love for me in Christ and His constant guidance through my growing/stretching times, I can trust Him to be with me and to always uplift me.

Dear Father,

Help me look forward to all the stretching and growing times that You provide me. Help me learn to approach them with the attitude, "What do You want to teach me through this?" Remind me daily of Your love, care, and forgiveness through Jesus. Amen.

Consider it pure joy, my brothers, whenever you face trials of many kinds, because you know that the testing of your faith develops perseverance. Perseverance must finish its work so that you may be mature and complete, not lacking anything.
James 1:2–4

I Will Do It

 icholas, you need to put your pajamas in the hamper." I held his pajamas out for him to take. "You do it." He pushed the pajamas away. "I have other chores to do. It is your job to put your pajamas in the hamper."

"Me not won to."

"Please put the pajamas in the hamper."

"I'll do it." Mark reached for the pajamas.

"Mark do it." Nicholas agreed.

"Thank you, Mark, but Nicholas needs to do this chore."

Doing the simple task would have been much easier for me than having the discussion with a 2-year-old about responsibility. But Nicholas needed to learn to put his pajamas away. Mark was just trying to help.

I am a helpful person too. If something needs to be done, I want to jump in and help. I don't always realize that by *not* doing something, it may give another person the opportunity to do that task. And maybe God is calling her instead of me for that position.

I felt a tremendous amount of guilt when I realized that I could not teach a Sunday school class anymore. I prayed that God would identify the person or persons to take the class. A difficult transition followed, but eventually God led a couple to volunteer to teach. Bob and Jan have continued to teach that class, and now Mark benefits from their early-childhood ministry.

There have been other times when I have been able to see how my no has allowed a special person the opportunity to serve God. A vacancy in a position could be just the nudge that someone needs to respond to God's call. I have to remember that just because something needs to be done, it does not mean that God is calling *me* to do it. He could be, and I have to prayerfully consider it, but He may be calling someone else. Then my "helpfulness" might be a hindrance to the person God really called. God may not want the job done nearly as much as He wants someone specific to do it.

Dear Father,

Sometimes I get carried away in wanting to do things for You and for others. Show me the areas in which You want me to do Your work. Keep me from getting sidetracked by what You want others to do. Amen.

There are different kinds of gifts,
but the same Spirit. There are different kinds
of service, but the same Lord. There are
different kinds of working, but the same God
works all of them in all men.
1 Corinthians 12:4–6

Trust

ark and Nicholas watched the children play in our front yard. Soon one child knocked on our door. "Can Mark and Nick come out and play?"

Mark knows to stay in our yard and that the street is off limits. While some of the children run into the street, Mark screeches to a stop with his toes just over the edge of the curb.

Nicholas knows that the street is absolutely forbidden. But when the neighborhood children move on to play in someone else's yard, he wants to move with them.

I walked out with Nicholas and told him, "You have to stay in our yard. Don't go anywhere else. Trust me. I know what is best for you."

I never go far from the window when I let the boys play in the front yard. They play with their friends while I fold laundry or work around the living room. When Nicholas took off down the street on the heels of one of his friends, I was outside just seconds later.

"Nicholas! Come here."

He came trotting back. "What?"

"You are done playing in the front yard today. You didn't trust and obey me. Go in the house."

"Me won play outside."

"You can play in the backyard."

"Not backyard."

"You didn't stay in our yard. Go in the house."

I also constantly cross the boundaries. I disobey God's laws. I forget to trust His promises to me. When I do, my Father brings me back "home" and reminds me of His rules. The Holy Spirit, living and working faith in me, helps me feel sorry for my disobedient actions and empowers me to confess my sins to my heavenly Father. I'm so thankful that my Father forgives me for Jesus' sake and that because of what Jesus did for me when He died on the cross, our Father/child relationship has no walls between us. God is always ready to welcome and guide me back to Him.

Dear Father,

Thank You for the blessings and the riches that You have given me. By the power of Your Spirit, help me trust Your promises to me and live as Your child in Your Kingdom. I praise and thank You for Your gracious forgiveness through Jesus, Your Son. Amen.

He [the Lord] cares for those who trust in Him.
Nahum 1:7

Mending Fences

 recent storm had taken a section of the fence down. Mark and Daddy set to work to repair it. Mark stood on the edge of the hole that Steve had just dug for the fence post. Dirt from under Mark's feet slid back into the hole. "Can I stand in the hole, Daddy?"

"The hole isn't big enough for you to stand in." Steve moved down and started digging another hole for the next post.

"Look, Daddy," Mark had moved down to the next hole with Steve. "I'm patting down this dirt that you're taking out of the hole. I'm helping you, Daddy."

"I see, Mark."

"I want to help, Daddy. What can I do to help?"

"You can take these boards and stack them over by the fence."

"Okay." Mark picked up a board, carried it to the spot Steve had indicated, then returned to Daddy. "I don't want to do that. That's not fun." He then found nails that Steve had removed from the fence and had placed in the wheelbarrow. "I'll hold these nails for you Daddy. That's how I'll help you." So Mark carried the nails around, with his head held high.

When Steve recounted this story for me I laughed.

"He wanted so much to help you, but carrying nails around didn't help you in the least."

"Sure it did. He didn't get in the way anymore."

That statement captured the spirit of Mark's helpfulness. Then I thought about myself. How willing am I to do what God asks of me? So often what really needs to be done isn't fun or glamorous; it may even be hard work. But to truly help God, I need to do what He asks me to do. Otherwise, I may realize that by doing what I thought needed to be done, I only stayed out of the way.

Dear Father,

Let me know what You want me to do. With the help of Your Spirit, I will do my best for You. Help me have a good attitude about the work You have given me, even if it is not fun. Amen.

I am the vine; you are the branches.
If a man remains in Me and I in him,
he will bear much fruit; apart from Me
you can do nothing.
John 15:5

We Need Five

e need five," Mark announced at lunch. "Five what?" I looked across the table at him. "Five in our family." He waited just long enough for his proclamation to sink in and then clarified it. "We need another kid."

"Would you like to pray for a baby, Mark?" I didn't have to nudge him. Mark immediately bowed his head and said, "Dear God, please put a baby in Mommy's tummy. Amen."

I was amused by Mark's request and pleased that he took his desire to God in prayer. Steve and I had discussed having another child, but we had decided it wasn't the right time. Now Mark prayed for a baby. He said something about the "new kid" and called him "he."

"What if God would give us a baby girl?" I asked.

Mark thought about it and then prayed, "Dear God, I want a baby girl. Amen."

I retold and laughed about this conversation until my positive pregnancy test a couple months later. Mark was the only one not surprised that we were going to have another baby. "I told God that I wanted a baby."

I wish I could say I prayed with that much confidence. Mark prayed, then waited, expecting God to answer his prayer. Quite often, I hesitate to take my requests to God. Sometimes I think God is concerned only with spiritual matters, not with the trivial things that I worry about. But the desires of my heart are not trivial to God. If one of my children needs or wants something, I do not see their need or request as trivial. He may not get it for a while, depending on circumstances, but his needs and desires are important to me.

God loves me and wants me to be happy. He may say no to me if my request will be harmful or if He has something better planned for me, but He always takes my needs and desires seriously. I can trust Him to always do and give what is best for me. He did just that when He gave His Son, Jesus, to save me from my sins.

Dear Father,

I sometimes feel like You are too busy with the big, important needs of people to be interested in my prayers. But You are my perfect, loving, heavenly Father. You always care about what I, Your child, need and want. Thank You for hearing my prayers and for answering with Your goodness each day. Thank You for supplying the greatest thing I'll ever need—my Savior, Jesus! Amen.

This is the confidence we have in approaching God: that if we ask anything according to His will, He hears us. And if we know that He hears us—whatever we ask—we know that we have what we asked of Him. 1 John 5:14–15

Hep Me

ou do it." Nicholas flung his pajamas onto my lap. "You can do it." I handed his sleeper back to him. Nicholas sat down and started working at getting his legs into his sleeper. "Hep me." I noticed the twisted toe. I gave the toe a little tug for a quick alignment.

Nicholas stood up and pulled the top part into place. He tried to put his hand in starting at the cuff. "Like this?" he asked.

"Start from the other side. Put your arm in here." I held the arm hole in position as he stuck his hand in.

"Where it go?" Nicholas turned around twice, looking for the other sleeve.

"Here it is. It was behind your back." I brought the other sleeve into position and held it in place just until he got his hand started in.

He slipped his arm in and pulled the zipper up. "I did it!" He paraded around the room, proud of his accomplishment.

"Yes, you did. Good job."

I could have whipped those pajamas on him in seconds. Nicholas struggled for 10 minutes. But during that time, he grew a bit. When he finished dressing for bed, he felt like he had accomplished something.

I constantly ask God for help—to make my problem go away, to fix it, to make it so I don't have to deal with it. My heavenly Father helps me help myself. He may allow me to struggle, but He assures me that I am not alone. God is right there with me, encouraging me, fixing the things that get twisted in my life, and helping me find what I need.

Knowing that God is always with me, even in the midst of my struggles, gives me the confidence to persevere even when things look too difficult. Believing that my heavenly Father gave me His ultimate help through the saving work of His Son, Jesus, I can trust Him to help me grow daily in faith and love toward Him.

Dear Father,

Thank You for staying with me and helping me when I can't handle something alone. Help me remember that You are always with me. Thank You for Your best help—my Savior, Jesus. Amen.

The Lord is with me; He is my helper. I will look in triumph on my enemies.
Psalm 118:7

Desus Luff Me

esus luff me, dis I know." I stopped talking to Mom and turned to look at Nicholas. "Fo da Bibo tell me so." I waved a hand to catch my mom's attention and nodded toward Nicholas. "Wittle ones to Him bewong. Day are weak but He is 'trong."

I grinned as Nicholas sang the refrain. I had not taught him that song. I had sung "Jesus Loves Me" to him on occasion, but not enough for him to learn it. He probably learned it in Sunday school.

I sing Bible songs, read Bible stories, pray with my children, and take their spiritual development seriously. I also appreciate the time other people spend sharing God's Word and love with my children in Sunday school and church.

One Sunday afternoon, Mark told me, "A boy wasted all of his dad's money and he had to eat *pig* food." This opened our discussion about the prodigal son and his forgiving father. We talked about what Mark had learned in Sunday school and how our heavenly Father is *our* forgiving Father.

God provides many teachers to help me learn more about Him—pastors, Bible-study leaders, friends, my husband, and our children. The Holy Spirit helps me learn more about God in everything I do and with everyone I meet.

I cannot automatically accept everything that I learn from others as the truth. I have learned to ask myself a question to help determine what God is trying to tell me. "How does what I learned here compare to what the Bible says?" The Bible is God's Word, the authority to which I turn for everyday living. As Nicholas' song reminds us "Fo da Bibo tell me so."

Dear Father,

Thank You for pastors, Sunday school teachers, and others in Christian education who spend hours preparing lessons for my children. Thank You also for my teachers, who share Your Word with me through Bible classes and in the daily living of their lives. Keep me open to what You would like to teach me through these people. Amen.

Fix these words of Mine in your hearts and minds; tie them as symbols on your hands and bind them on your foreheads. Teach them to your children,
talking about them when you sit at home and when you walk along the road,
when you lie down and when you get up.
Deuteronomy 11:18–19.

Preparations

I surveyed the room that in five years had been transformed from an office into a playroom and now would become a nursery. I thought that with a little cleaning out, we could re-arrange the boys' bedroom to house most of their toys and leave the baby toys in the nursery.

As I looked at the bare wall, I envisioned a crib next to it, and I could picture the rocking chair in the corner. I can repaint that chest and put the baby's things in there. And since Tennie has been wanting to help me stencil, we could stencil designs on the chest and the crib too. The new baby's room was coming together in my mind.

I shuddered and thought, I'll need to get rid of that chunky old bookcase. It won't fit in the room with all the baby stuff. I want the room to be perfect.

I am getting excited about having another baby! One of the ways that I am preparing for his or her arrival is by fixing up a nursery. I have been bringing in things from when Mark and Nicholas were babies, taking inventory of what we will need, and watching the sales on baby items. By the time this little one arrives, we will have a charming nursery.

Out of His great love and for Jesus' sake, God promises all believers a new life—full of joy and glory—when we die. God is preparing a place for me—a beautiful place in heaven. Even if I spent unlimited funds and decorated until all my dreams came true, this little nursery would not begin to compare to the beautiful grand home that Jesus will take me to when I go to live with Him in heaven.

Dear Father,

I cannot imagine what You have planned for me! Streets of gold and gates with pearls are beyond my comprehension. But I know from the descriptions in Your Word that heaven will be glorious. Being with You will be the most glorious of all. Thank You for giving me the hope of living in heaven through Jesus Christ's death and resurrection. Amen.

In my Father's house are many rooms; if it were not so, I would have told you. I am going there to prepare a place for you.
John 14:2

Knighthood

sat in the playroom doorway and began grouping the boy's toys. I had threatened to clean this room for weeks. The time had finally come. I would throw out the junk and pack away the toys the boys hadn't played with recently.

Mark stood beside me. "Mommy, why don't you put away the toys that we don't play with." He had heard my threats.

"I will. Help me by telling me what you don't play with anymore."

"The knight. I don't play with the knight." I turned and looked at my son. He seemed serious. Was he saying that for shock value? If so, it worked.

(When he first got his knight set, he acted as if there were no other toys in the world. He took it everywhere. He studied the brochure that came with it and made lists of accessories he wanted, one of which was a castle. I had considered getting Mark the castle for Christmas. I planned on watching how he played with the pieces he had.)

"Well, I'm glad I didn't get you the castle then."

"Uh-huh." Then he realized what I had said, "Oh ... I want the castle."

"I'm not going to buy you something that big that you

may not play with very often. Do you think you may be growing out of your knight toys?"

God's gifts to us may seem small and insignificant at first. But with use, they can grow and become a collection of a variety of His gifts to us.

If I neglect the gifts that God gives to me, they may not grow. God has not given me gifts to hide in the closet, rather He would help me develop these gifts. I can trust Him to help me identify His gifts to me. I can ask Him to help me use these gifts to glorify Him.

Dear Father,

Thank You for the gifts that You have given me. Help me to identify other gifts You have given me. Thank You for Your best gift of all—salvation through Christ Jesus. Encourage me as I use and develop Your gifts to me. Give me courage and joy to share the Good News of Jesus with the people around me. Amen.

Each one should use whatever gift he has received to serve others, faithfully administering God's grace in its various forms.
1 Peter 4:10

The gift of God is eternal life in Christ Jesus our Lord.
Romans 6:23

Valentines

gathered the supplies Mark and I needed to make Valentines. Then we sat down at the kitchen table together to create the Valentines for the children in his preschool class. I opened a bag of candy conversation hearts. "We can make valentines and have some candy while we are working."

Mark was excited about the whole idea. He worked hard at printing his name. I spelled his friend's names, showing Mark how to make some of the letters he did not know. All the while, we munched on candy.

Mark began to tire halfway through the 13 names, and when Nicholas woke up, I put the project away for a few days. We finished the Valentines during our second session. Mark was very pleased with his accomplishments and so was I.

This task turned out to be fun, though it could have been a major headache. I knew that this was a project that would push Mark to the limit, and he might not want to even try. I tried to help by sitting right next to him, encouraging him when he started to get frustrated or tired, and making the experience as pleasant as possible.

There are times when God puts me in a situation that seems to push me to my limit. At those times, I can take comfort in knowing that I am not alone. God is right there with me, encouraging me. When I feel like I want to give up, He lifts me up through the kind words of a friend or with an indication that I am on the right track.

He may even enable me to set the task aside for a while and come back to it when I am rested. God reminds me through the Holy Spirit that I am not alone. When I am done, I know that I have accomplished something with God's help.

Dear Father,

Thank You for always being with me, especially when I have a difficult task to undertake. Let me know that You are beside me, and lift me up when I feel like I cannot continue. I rely on Your presence and power to carry me through the hills and the valleys of my life. Amen.

May our Lord Jesus Christ Himself and God our Father, who loved us and by His grace gave us eternal encouragement and good hope, encourage your hearts and strengthen you in every good deed and word.
2 Thessalonians 2:16–17

Good News

ark fiddled with the car stereo, trying to find the beginning of the tape. "Mommy got sandbox," Nicholas announced from the backseat. I smiled. Mark had been at preschool when Nicholas and I went to the toy store.

Mark, too busy to listen, kept working with the stereo. Nicholas knew that he had good news, so he repeated, "Mommy got sandbox."

Mark continued to fiddle, then stopped. "What did he say?"

Nicholas had the opportunity to share his news for the third time. Then Mark turned to me. "Did you?"

I smiled and nodded.

"What kind of sandbox? Is the sand already in it?" I answered his questions as Nicholas delighted in informing his brother of the good news.

I learned something about sharing the Gospel from this exchange. My friend may hear my Good News several times before he or she begins to listen. It feels frustrating to not be heard the first or second time, but the steps I take are valuable. My words may lay the groundwork and prepare my friend for the next person's message of God's love and forgiveness through Jesus.

When I don't see immediate results from my witness, it doesn't mean that my message had no effect. Like Nicholas, I may not be as articulate as another person, but the message that I have to share is still valuable. It is God's Good News for all people! I need to keep sharing this Good News, and even though I don't notice any change, the Holy Spirit may be using my words to open and soften my friend's heart.

Dear Father,

Help me recognize the people with whom You would have me share Your love and my faith. Even if I don't ever see any results, help me to not be discouraged. Affirm to me that Your Holy Spirit is at work in this person's life. Amen.

As the rain and the snow come down from heaven, and do not return to it without watering the earth and making it bud and flourish, so that it yields seed for the sower and bread for the eater, so is My word that goes out from My mouth: It will not return to Me empty, but will accomplish what I desire and achieve the purpose for which I sent it.
Isaiah 55:10–11

Thank You

"Duice, Mommy, me won duice." Nicholas stood beside my bed. I opened my eyes and looked at him. "Nicholas, why don't you crawl in bed and cuddle with Mommy for a little bit." I lifted the covers and hoped I could rest for a few more minutes.

"No, me firsty. Me won duice. Come, Mommy."

"Okay, I'll get you some juice." I crawled out of bed and staggered toward the kitchen.

"Carry me." Nicholas reached his arms toward me.

"Carry you? I feel like I can barely walk myself."

"Carry."

"Why don't you carry me?"

"You too big. I wittle."

I smiled and slid my hands under his arms, swinging him onto my hip. As he came to a rest, I heard him say, "Thank you."

Wow! I hadn't expected Nicholas to thank me. It felt so good to hear his words! In the warm glow of being thanked—of not being taken for granted—I "floated" all the way to the kitchen with Nicholas in my arms.

Before this, I had never considered how my thanks might affect God. I was brought up to thank God for the blessings that I notice, and especially for the gift of Jesus, our Savior. But just as a child might not think about his parents needing thanks, I thought that God didn't *need* my thanks. God doesn't *need* anything! But I also realized that God desires my praise and thanks.

When Jesus healed the ten men of leprosy, only one came back to say thanks. Jesus asked, "Were not all ten cleansed? Where are the other nine?" He expected all of the men to thank Him and desired their praise and thanks. I don't want to get too busy enjoying my blessings that I forget to take the time to say thank You to the one who blesses me each day with His love, care, and forgiveness.

Dear Father,

Thank You! Thank You for Your constant presence in my life and for the many ways that You provide for me and bless me. As Mark says at the end of his prayers, "Thank You for everything." Thank You especially for Jesus, my Savior. Amen.

Enter His gates with thanksgiving and His courts with praise; give thanks to Him and praise His name. For the Lord is good and His love endures forever; His faithfulness continues through all generations.
Psalm 100:4–5

145

Vision

ark crawled in bed with me, giving us a chance to cuddle and talk before we started our day. The talk turned to one of Mark's favorite subjects, the baby. "I wish I could see the baby!"

"I know, I would like to see it too." I rubbed his hair. "You know what? The doctor has a special camera that takes a picture of the baby while it is still inside Mommy. Then we can see the baby a little bit, but it is not a very good picture. Would you like to go with us if we have that done?"

"Yeah!" I could see he was thinking. "Will the baby be wearing clothes or no clothes?"

"No clothes," I answered.

"Then we will be able to see if it is a boy or a girl?"

"Maybe. But even the doctors can't always tell. We can't see much."

Later that day, I got out Mark's baby book and found his sonogram pictures. I wanted him to know that it would not be like looking at a snapshot. "Here is a picture of you, Mark. Can you see your head?"

"No."

"Here it is, and here is your arm going around, and you are sucking your thumb." He grinned, but he did not see any of it. I could not see it at first either. All of the various parts had to be pointed out to me, and then I began identifying them myself.

The Bible is full of descriptions of God and heaven. But I still do not really know what God is like. A sonogram picture seems a lot like my picture of God. At first, I really could not see God. Then with help, I was able to identify characteristics and see images of Him. But still, I cannot see Him clearly.

Just as I will not be able to really see my baby until it is born, it will not be until I get to heaven that I will be able to really see God, face to face. Then I will know God in all of His glory and majesty.

Dear Father,

Even though my knowledge of You is limited, I know enough to look forward to seeing You face to face and getting to know You more fully. What I know of You now only begins to scratch the surface of how wonderful You really are. Amen.

Now we see but a poor reflection
as in a mirror; then we shall see face to face.
Now I know in part; then I shall know fully,
even as I am fully known.
1 Corinthians 13:12

Hope

 stumbled over Nicholas as I tried to move to the refrigerator to get some eggs and milk. "Sweetie, Mommy is trying to make a special breakfast, but it is hard to do with you right under my feet."

He did not say anything, he just whined for attention. Then he clung to my leg as I measured the flour into the blender. "Mark is playing with the farm. Why don't you play with him, and then we can have a special breakfast?"

I was about to get out my baking pan when I hit on an idea. I went to the pantry and got out the syrup. "Nicholas, can you put this on the table for Mommy?"

Before he even looked up, he started shaking his head. Then he caught a glimpse of the syrup. With a big grin on his face he reached for the bottle. He bounced across the kitchen and set it in the middle of the table.

Mark came in the kitchen and spotted the syrup. "Are we having pancakes?" Mark's smile was almost as big as his brother's.

"No, we're having Dutch babies. They are not pancakes, but they are like pancakes."

"All right!" Then he disappeared into the living room, and Nicholas went with him.

Nicholas still did not know what "Dutch babies" or "special breakfast" meant. But the syrup bottle offered him hope. He now believed that I had something good in store for him.

God has something good in store for me too. Like Nicholas, I do not have a full grasp of what God has planned, but He has provided me with something from which my hope stems and something on which to base my faith.

God gave me the Bible so I would have hope in things that I have not seen, things that are beyond my comprehension, and things that are to come. Like the syrup bottle, it is but a glimpse of what God has planned for me. But it gives me hope because it gives me an idea of what to expect.

Dear Father,

Thank You for the Bible and the hope that is mine through Your Word. When I start to feel swallowed up by the hopelessness of this world, remind me to turn to the Scriptures for encouragement and direction. Amen.

For everything that was written in the past
was written to teach us, so that through
endurance and the encouragement of the
Scriptures we might have hope.
Romans 15:4

Promises

 brushed my teeth, washed my face, and went through my nightly ritual. When I finished getting ready for bed, I went to the boys' bedroom. I slipped the blankets out from under Nicholas' legs and pulled the covers up to his chin. I stroked his blond hair and kissed his cheek. "I love you," I whispered even though I knew he could not hear me.

Then I moved to Mark's bed. I tugged the covers out from underneath him and pulled them over his body. Then I crawled in bed next to Mark and stroked his face and his brown, wavy hair. Earlier that evening, when I tucked him in, he asked that I lay with him when I went to bed.

This is a common request of both the boys that I really do not understand. Usually by the time I go to bed, they are not even awake. So they are asking for something that they will not even be able to appreciate. I could just agree to their request and then go to bed. But if I make a promise to my children, I keep it, even if they do not know that I am being faithful to them. The trust relationship I have with my children is too valuable for me to not take it seriously.

God is faithful to me and His promises are sure. I have no way of holding God accountable, but I do not have to. He keeps His promises to me, even if I have no way of knowing that He is being faithful. I can feel confident in His faithfulness because He has already established a reputation of trustworthiness.

So many of God's promises are not fulfilled until generations later. The people He made His original promise to often don't see the outcome, but they do know that with God it will come to pass, just as He said it would. I know that when God decides the time is right, Jesus will return in glory and take me to heaven to live with Him. I know because God promised.

Dear Father,

You are faithful and true, and I do not have to doubt that You will follow through on Your promises. Give me a confident trust in Your promises and Your actions. Amen.

The Lord is faithful to all His promises and
loving toward all He has made.
Psalm 145:13

Who Are You?

 pushed the door open and strode to the back of the little store, headed for the stamps. Nicholas ran after me, screaming. He managed to get in front of my legs. I stepped around him and kept going.

When we got to the mini post office, I paused in line while Nicholas screamed and pawed me. As I handed my money to the clerk, another customer turned to Nicholas and said, "What's wrong, honey?"

I answered for him. "He wants to be carried." She frowned and her eyes narrowed as she looked at me, but she said nothing else.

We left in much the same manner as we entered the store. After I got Nicholas settled in his car seat, I turned and saw the same lady getting into her car. I noticed her watching Nicholas. The expression on her face seemed to say, "That poor little boy. Why won't his mother just carry him if that is all he wants?"

I got in my car and drove off. I probably did appear pretty heartless. This woman could not see that I had carried him all morning. She could not see that just prior to entering the store, Nicholas had demanded, even ordered, me to carry him. She could not see that I was trying to teach my child a little bit of self-reliance or that screaming is not an effective tool in getting your way. I was trying to do what was best for my child, regardless of how it looked to a stranger.

At times, I have judged other people only by what I could see. I haven't taken into account factors that were not apparent to me. I may have felt that I knew a better way. I have even questioned God's reasoning. I may see a situation and even pray about it. I feel like I know what needs to be done, but God does not act accordingly. Like the woman, I am looking in from the outside. I do not have the same information that God has. He is going to do what is best for His children, regardless of how it looks to me or anyone else.

Dear Father,

You know so much more about me than I know about myself. You know what is best for me even if I think it is catastrophic. Help me trust You to take care of me, knowing that You love me dearly. Amen.

But who are you, O man, to talk back to God?
"Shall what is formed say to him who formed it,
'Why did you make me like this?'" Does not the
potter have the right to make out of the same
lump of clay some pottery for noble purposes
and some for common use?
Romans 9:20–21

Beautiful Memories

ook over here at the tickle bird. The tickle bird is going to get you. Watch out. Here it comes." The photographer moved her stuffed bird in to nuzzle each of the boys. She pulled back and snapped the picture in the midst of their giggles.

My big hams were having a great time posing for the camera. They looked so adorable with smiles on their faces, sitting in the various positions in which the photographer posed them. The scene had been different just moments before. The boys had been bickering and fighting over a toy.

Two years ago, we took Mark to have his picture taken. At that time, photo sessions were worse than vegetables for Mark. We tried everything to get at least a pleasant look out of him. Finally, Steve stood on his head in the corner of the studio. Mark laughed just long enough for the photographer to snap his picture. It is one of the best pictures we have of Mark.

I have gone to extremes to preserve memories of the children as they grow up. Not just any memories but wonderful memories, even if they are a bit contrived.

A friend of mine said that she thinks people have amnesia about the bad times. I think she is right. I want to remember the happy times and am more willing to let the painful times dissolve from my memory. When I sit in my rocking chair with a grandchild and recall stories about when Daddy was a little boy, I will remember this time with only fondness.

It will probably be the same on Judgment Day when God looks at my life. He will look at me through Christ's blood, and it will be as if He has amnesia about all the bad times. My husband may have stood on his head to help us preserve beautiful memories, but Jesus died on the cross so that I could appear blameless before my Father at the end of time.

Dear Father,

The beauty You have created covers everything, even the ugliness in my life. Thank You for loving me so much that You went to the extremes to preserve me. Amen.

For all have sinned and fall short of the
glory of God, and are justified freely
by His grace through the redemption
that came by Christ Jesus.
Romans 3:23–24

A Parting Thought

Be imitators of God, therefore, as dearly
loved children and live a life of love, just as
Christ loved us and gave Himself up for us
as a fragrant offering and sacrifice to God.
Ephesians 5:1–2